Your First Garden

A Landscape Primer for New Home Owners

Judith Adam

FIREFLY BOOKS

A FIREFLY BOOK

Published by Firefly Books Ltd. 2016
Copyright © 2016 Firefly Books Ltd.
Text copyright © 2016 Judith Adam

First printing

Publisher Cataloging-in-Publication Data (U.S.)

Adam, Judith, author.
Your first garden / Judith Adam.
Richmond Hill, Ontario, Canada : Firefly Books, 2016. Includes index.
Summary: "Ideal for new homeowners in the suburbs, this guidebook takes gardening style into account as it covers all the unique ways to make a yard more welcoming"
ISBN 978-1-77085-708-7 (pbk.)
Backyard gardens. Landscape gardening.
SB473.A336   712.6 – dc23

Library and Archives Canada Cataloguing in Publication

Adam, Judith, author
Your first garden / Judith Adam.
Includes index.
ISBN 978-1-77085-708-7 (paperback)
1. Gardening—Handbooks, manuals, etc. I. Title.
SB450.97.A43 2016   635   C2015-908182-3

Published in the United States by
Firefly Books (U.S.) Inc.
P.O. Box 1338, Ellicott Station
Buffalo, New York 14205

Published in Canada by
Firefly Books Ltd.
50 Staples Avenue, Unit 1
Richmond Hill, Ontario L4B 0A7

Cover and interior design: Hartley Millson

Printed in China

The publisher gratefully acknowledges the financial support for our publishing program by the Government of Canada through the Canada Book Fund as administered by the Department of Canadian Heritage.

Table of Contents

Introduction

YOU'VE JUST MADE ONE OF THE MOST IMPORTANT AND MOST expensive investments of your life—you've bought a brand-new house with a non-existent garden. What's next?

As a new homeowner, you want to feel confident that you've made a smart decision. While it may be a temptation to imagine that the exterior footage is not part of the house's purchase value, the reality is, you've paid for every square foot of property. Making plans and decisions about landscaping that property will ratify your purchase and ensure that you take full advantage of all the assets you've acquired.

Failing to make landscape plans, on the other hand, is a lot like writing off that third bedroom or an unfinished basement—ignoring space that initially seems useless or confusing. Landscaping "seals the deal" by providing your new house with context, making it look appropriate in the landscape—and that in turn reflects on the smartness of the purchase and the value for money paid. It also presents a full picture of the home's potential, in both the near and distant future.

The purpose of home landscaping is to provide an intelligent, useful and attractive setting for your home. Pride of ownership begins on day one, and regardless of how much time you plan to invest in the house itself, you'll want it to look terrific from the get-go and will work toward that for the first couple of years. It's all about figuring out how to make the exterior garden work with your home and planning the outdoor space so that it will be useful and functional for specific purposes—providing access to entrances, paths for getting around, and areas for dining and relaxation, entertainment, sports activities, and so forth.

The truth is, much of the foundation of good landscape planning is simply rational thinking: learning how to divide space, how to determine essential and practical uses and how to make changes

Landscape planning always begins with an objective assessment of the site and a list of its assets and debits.

The process of house construction removes topsoil, so expect to purchase fresh soil before you plant.

and choices in all the areas of your property, from the front lawn and entrance to the private spaces in the backyard and the areas along the driveway and sides of the house. Increasing your property's beauty is an important goal of a landscape plan, but equally important is making sure that all the features of your lot function as they should. For example, water must drain away from the house, the entrance walkway needs to be wider than a one-person bachelor path, and seating areas should be screened for privacy.

Every property has its challenges, and landscape planning always starts with an objective assessment of the site, during which the owner creates a list of its assets and debits, noticing what features are inadequate or unattractive. Are slopes too steep to walk on safely? Is there a secure space for garbage cans and an air conditioner unit? Are the pathways level and firm? Learning to evaluate the options is just as important as getting the job done well. Then you have to balance those needs against a realistic projection of how you would like to use the space and how much money you're willing to invest to make that happen. Resolving what you have with what you want is a giant leap toward designing a landscape to meet your needs.

Landscaping a New Home

That said, whether a new house is built in a new subdivision or in an established neighborhood, there's a good chance that it

will lack even the most rudimentary landscaping features such as trees and shrubs. The lawn may be new sod that has been laid over a minimal layer of topsoil, or there may be no sod at all. You have a clean site to work with—and a clear invitation to build from the ground up.

It's often the case that gardening careers begin in small ways, with the planting of a few flowers or vegetables just outside the back door. Plants of every kind are inevitably the most prominent features in your garden, and they are also the most complex and diverse. As living components of the landscape, their value is more than aesthetic—they create a healthy and rewarding context for your outdoor activities. That's why understanding their cultural needs—soil quality, moisture and light—is an important key to plant selection and a crucial step toward successful landscape planning.

As the garden grows, small gestures soon lead to larger efforts and increasing rewards. Landscape planning is the logical extension of gardening, and you're probably doing it in your mind already. Most imagined improvements and attempted changes reflect your interest in developing the garden landscape. This book is meant to encourage and support those interests and show the way to effective decision making.

Take a good look at your yard today, because it's going to change and grow with this book.

A brand-new house means the start of something big—made even better with a beautiful landscaping plan.

Successful Landscape Planning Requires an Understanding of

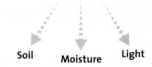

Soil   Moisture   Light

Adding Value & Enjoyment

THERE ARE GOOD REASONS FOR LANDSCAPING, WHETHER small or large, and they all start with space and function. The essential questions are these: How can we make this an attractive space we're proud of? How can we make it suit our needs? How can we create a place for the special interests of family members and guests? Is there room for a vegetable garden or a hot tub? Is there a patio or deck to accommodate outdoor furniture, where we can sit and eat pleasantly outdoors with privacy from neighbors?

Landscaping should add to the value of your property. Good choices in landscape development always reveal the thoughtful intent of the gardener. Dividing your plans into phases over a three-to-five-year period is the best way to make sure they're both affordable and doable. Each phase should be finished and have the appearance of completion before another step begins, allowing you to temporarily rest and save additional funds before you take the next step.

Be sure your landscaping improvements are likely to be saleable to a future buyer. The more expensive and permanent the landscaping development, the more necessary it is to ensure its lasting value and broad appeal. Swimming pools, for example, are the particular passion of many, though not all, people, but if your neighborhood contains many properties with swimming

Landscaping should add to the value of your property.

pools, there may be an established acceptance that pools are desirable. Nevertheless, think before you leap into pool projects, and never install a pool that requires more than half the available garden space.

Before you customize your property and make it the fulfillment of personal dreams, be sure you intend to stick around and enjoy it for some time. Regardless of what your investment may be, you can expect the curb appeal of a well-landscaped garden to add as much as 10 percent to the value of your property, provided the changes you make are reasonable, enhancing and appealing to most residents on your street.

In an undeveloped new subdivision, you could potentially spend one to two thousand dollars importing the soil and mulch you'll need to establish garden beds and spaces for shrubs and trees.

The simple ratio of one thousand dollars' worth of development for each year you expect to remain on the property works well for short-term planning. For five thousand dollars spent in the garden, you should hope to enjoy the changes for five years to get your value from the investment.

Planning a Landscape

A landscape plan should be based on thoughtful consideration of what is necessary and useful in developing your new yard's potential. Your goal is not to produce a site worthy of a magazine article. Instead, you should be making decisions about how to enhance the value of your home, even as you make your yard into a place in which your family and friends want to spend more time.

Putting It Down on Paper

Make a rough conceptual drawing that reflects the current state of affairs in your yard. Show the house, the garage, trees, patios and walkways, if they exist. Then sketch in perennial beds, foundations beds, trees and shrubs and any other items on your wish list (a play area for young children?). You've now got the basic plan, and you can make photocopies to experiment with. Keep the plan up to date as changes are made to the yard. That way,

You can expect the curb appeal of a well-landscaped garden to add as much as 10 percent to the value of your property.

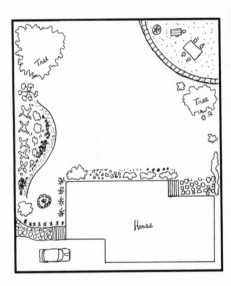

Commit your plan to paper, and make copies to experiment with as new ideas develop.

Ten-Point Assessment Survey

When landscaping a new yard for the first time, use these questions to identify your yard's potential challenges, determine the changes you want to make, and order them in priority.

1. Size and shape

What are the dimensions of your yard? Is it rectangular, square, irregular? Does it have unusual proportions—is it long and narrow, wide and shallow? Does it have sharp angles? If the size is too large, can it be divided? If it's too small, can it be made to appear more spacious?

2. Boundaries

Is the perimeter defined with a wall, fence or hedge? How is the front yard separated from the street? Is it visually clear where private property begins? How are the boundaries between neighbors indicated? How close are the neighbors on three sides? Is there any kind of privacy barrier or screening in place; is it needed?

3. Patios and decks

Do they exist? If not, are they on your wish list?

4. The lawn

Is the grass healthy, thick and deep green? If you've been in the house for a winter season, have you noticed whether the lawn drains quickly after snow melts? Are there areas worn thin by constant foot traffic?

5. Irrigation

Other than by rain, how is the garden watered? Is there an in-ground irrigation system—for the lawn only? For the planting beds? Do you plan to water with a movable hose and sprinkler attachment?

6. Entrances and pathways

How many entrances are there to the yard? If there's a back fence, does it have a gate? Is there a pathway alongside the garage? How wide is the path? Do you want to improve steps and paths with wood, concrete, paving bricks or natural stone?

7. Side strips

Are there strips of land alongside the house, driveway or garage walls? How are they surfaced? Does any strip of land serve as a pathway entrance to the yard? Do walls of the house or garage have room for vines?

8. Growing areas

How can you best place garden beds so that they can be enjoyed from seating areas, entrances and doors and from inside through window views?

9. Trees and shade

If there are existing trees, do they produce dense shade, filtered light or dappled light? Are any trees growing on public property by the roadside? In your community, are there bylaws governing pruning and removal of trees on private property?

10. The garage and driveway

Is the garage a prominent feature of the property? Does it have a window and a planted window box? If the driveway is asphalt, is it banded with cobblestones or another kind of ornamental stone?

you'll have a record of your progress as well as an illustration of projects yet to be incorporated.

Developing a Vision

Gardens are personal places. Making a garden is a rare license to create the world as you would have it, to reflect your temperament and philosophy in the landscape you call your own.

Your attitude toward your interior space may reflect your outside aesthetic as well. Are you a stickler for order in your house or do you take a more relaxed view? Carefully organized closets with everything in place could translate to a more structured garden style, with formal entrances and seating areas, balanced borders and plants chosen for their stately form and well-defined lines. Boxwood hedges, for example, would make good space organizers in such a garden, along with standard rose trees and stone urns.

On the other hand, disorganized drawers may translate into a preference for a relaxed garden setting, with naturalized areas of mixed perennial plantings and cascading shrubs. This informal garden might have collections of large hostas under Japanese maples and an area for spring bloodroot, bleeding hearts, primulas and forget-me-nots among lilac, hydrangea and mock orange shrubs.

The question to ask is not so much what you want, but rather what kind of environment makes you feel secure, able to relax? What balance of order and chaos centers your thoughts? What forms, textures and colors are consistently pleasing? The gardens we make ourselves are hopefully in our own image, our own profile expressed in a handmade living landscape. A bit of self-obsession doesn't go amiss in the garden.

User-Friendly Gardens

First and foremost, consider who uses the garden and for what purpose. If children with play equipment and kiddy pools are part of the action, be sure to factor them into the plan. Since all children know that basketball is the most important use of a driveway, why not relegate athletic activities to the front yard, where a low fence or hedge can help to keep equipment in bounds

First and foremost, consider who uses the garden and for what purpose.

yet still allow passers-by to gather and enjoy the game.

The interests of flower growers and vegetable growers can be negotiated with great charm in a cottage garden planting. Combining Shasta daisies and delphiniums with tomatoes and currants appeals to all the senses. Almost every perennial plant and flowering shrub pairs well with food plants chosen for their attractive display. Purple-leaf sand cherry with ruby Swiss chard at its feet, bleeding heart with a skirt of Italian lettuce and hydrangea flanked with red pear tomatoes are some of the colorful combinations of mixed plantings.

Privacy and retreat are also important needs to be considered. A quiet place for reading and the occasional nap should always be available. Building in a small seating place at the back of the garden to accommodate a bench or two chairs will give you a reason to stop work and enjoy the view of your favorite plants. Even a hammock strung between two trees is an opportunity to simply enjoy being in the garden with no particular task at hand except contemplation of the sky.

Before You Begin Work

Before you start, consider any permissions, permits and clearances your work might require. If you want to build a fence on a lot line, you'll have to negotiate this with the neighbor or build on your own side within the line. Some cities and regions have few restrictions on landscaping, while others may send inspectors around with regularity. Building permits may be required for structural work like parking pads, decks and patios. If you want to plant a front hedge, you'll need to check how close it can be to the public pavement. Be sure to call all utility services to have underground lines located. You'll also need to locate gas lines, and keep in mind that newer subdivisions may also have buried electrical power lines.

Moving Mountains: Who Does the Work?

Moving countless wheelbarrows of soil, digging new beds, planting perennials, shrubs and trees, lawn mowing and composting all require familiar skills. You may be proficient at one and more of an amateur at another, but these accomplishments are

Trees
Trees planted near the house should be carefully chosen for size and shape. Select small trees with limited foliage that will fit into the scale of the garden and not overwhelm the house.

Architectural Features
Even small architectural features like this bird house can add scale and interest to a garden.

Shrubs
Use evergreens with upright conical or pyramidal forms that fit into the available space in front and side gardens.

Plants
Plants add color and interest when they bloom. Try to select a mixture of annuals and perennials that bloom at different times so that there is always color in the garden.

Borders
A border of stones provides a clear division between the lawn and the garden and is an attractive architectural feature in its own right.

Elements of Landscape Design

Sometimes the best landscaping results evolve gradually as you develop design and building techniques. Above all, plan thoughtfully and don't rush. Below are some guidelines about style, structure, plant material and color selection that will help get you thinking.

Personal style

Most of us know what we like, and that's a good thing. But if you don't have a clear sense of your outdoor preferences, feel free to take a look at some magazines and gardening books or watch a few television gardening shows. Get comfortable with what you find appealing and what's possible before you start.

Planning

Good planning is based on an objective assessment of the site conditions. What will work in your yard? Do you have space for large objects such as a deck, a hot tub, a swimming pool or a double garage? By identifying what is possible, reasonable and achievable, you can create guidelines for a practical design plan, one that takes into account available light, soil and the grade of your property.

Planting style

Plants can be used in groups and clusters to effectively cover space in a mass or with less density and more focus on detail and individual profile. English cottage gardens or woodland themes are based on massed plants that cover a lot of ground. Japanese and southwestern themes are more sparing in their use of plant material, with less density and more individual specimen plants.

Succession planting

Flowering trees and shrubs and herbaceous perennial plants provide blossoms, texture and scent that are important features of each season. All too often the majority of floral display comes in spring and early summer. With research and planning, your garden can include plants that demonstrate their ornamental value throughout the growing season, including the later months, when gardens can be exclusively green.

Color choices

Color is the most personal element of garden design and can influence how the garden is used and enjoyed. The colors of perennial and annual plants and bulbs can change with the seasons. Various areas of the garden can be planted with differing color schemes, all in the same season. Woody plants with purple leaves contribute a depth and richness to the landscape. Variegated plants with green and white or cream leaves bring light to shady areas, and gold or chartreuse foliage contributes interest and diversity. Conifers also come in colors such as blue-green, steel blue, gray and gold.

Architectural features

Almost any kind of hard construction has architectural value in the garden. The most familiar objects are walkways and benches, fences and gates, trellises and pergolas, arbors and ponds. Small objects such as birdbaths and statuary are useful for punctuating entrances and creating local interest within a planting bed. But too many architectural objects can disrupt the flow of garden areas and confuse the design intent. The best guideline is to be sure that each object has functional or artistic merit.

Garden bones

Prominent woody plants and architectural structures such as fences, gates, steps, trellises and arbors are the bones of the garden and form a permanent structure through the changing seasons. Imagine the garden as it will appear in the coldest part of the winter, and use that as a baseline for determining where to plant trees or evergreen shrubs, build a wall or place a birdbath.

Scale and balance

Understanding the scale of the garden helps plants and trees to appear natural in their setting. A large garden can accommodate spreading trees and shrubs in mass plantings. Dwarf shrubs and pyramidal trees are more in scale for a small garden, with individual specimen plants for accent. The elements of the garden—vertical trees and shrubs, horizontal lawns and groundcovers, hard stone surfaces and architectural structures—should be in balance, or in "agreement," with the available space.

A Landscape Planning Checklist

❏ **Determine** your priorities for work to be accomplished this season. Include improvements to make the garden more useable, as well as special wish-list items.

❏ **Prepare** a drawing of the garden as it is and indicate the changes you want to make.

❏ **Make** a time-line plan indicating start and completion dates for each phase of the project, showing where some tasks might overlap to save time.

❏ **Apply** for building permits if necessary.

❏ **Establish** a budget for the entire project as well as for each phase.

❏ **Research** and locate building materials and plants.

❏ **Find** contractors for projects that require special skills, for example, underground irrigation, deck building and brick laying.

❏ **Call** utility companies to locate and mark buried service lines.

❏ **Notify** neighbors of the work schedule.

❏ **Outline** the shape of new planting beds and prepare soil with organic materials.

❏ **Plant** trees, shrubs, hedges and perennials.

❏ **Install** new sod lawn if necessary.

generally within the abilities of most homeowners. Now, however, you may be considering tasks you have seen carried out but haven't attempted on your own. You might enjoy standing at the side of a construction site and watching the progress, but that doesn't qualify you for construction work. Could you figure out the basics of soil grading, understand how to fit interlock bricks together, select and install large-scale nursery plants? Or should you be looking for a professional service to carry out your plans?

Some skills are the specific domain of traditional trades like bricklayers and stonemasons, and with good reasons. Laying a dry brick pathway with sand in the joints requires more thought than skill, but building a mortared brick wall requires a depth of experience best left to professional bricklayers. Similarly, fitting together a patio of straight-edged flagstone is not very complicated, but making a patio of flagstone with irregular shapes requires the stone-cutting skills of a mason. Taking on jobs that are beyond your abilities is a waste of time and materials.

When planning your first garden try to think of how the area will look once the plants have had a chance to mature. In this mature garden the front walkway is bordered by plants of different heights and colors to add variety. The tree provides cooling shade to the house and lawn and the container plants on either side of the driveway softens the expanse of concrete.

Calling for Help

Sometimes it's smart to hire experts to get parts of the job done quickly. Professional landscapers have a large fund of experience, and you should select one who is generous with his or her time. There's much to be gained by listening to their advice, as well as their cautions, and involving them in reaching final decisions. Landscape contractors want to leave you with a pleasing and long-lasting installation. After all, their business depends on you giving friends and colleagues glowing referrals.

Your contractor should supply you with a written cost estimate that details how many plants will be supplied, their Latin botanical names, plant sizes and costs. Necessary amounts of soil, shredded bark and foundation materials should be specified in cubic yards; sizes and kinds of stone and lumber should be noted. Agree on start and completion dates, although some delays may be unavoidable. Be prepared to pay a deposit up front before work begins, and provide washroom facilities for anyone working on your property.

2. Soil Basics

IF YOU'RE MYSTIFIED BY THE WORKINGS OF SOIL AND THINKING OF skipping this section, please don't. The growth potential of your perennial plants and flowering shrubs is dependent on the quality of soil in which they're growing. Understanding how to give plants the soil they need for a long and healthy life is what makes the difference between rapid growth and slow decline. Learning how soil works isn't difficult or boring. When you understand that the success of expensive purchased plants (or your own tender seedlings, should you decide to start your own plants) is determined by the quality of your garden soil, you'll want to know more about what's going on under your feet.

We appreciate shrubs and perennial plants most when they're in bloom or offering ornamental foliage display. But these plants are still alive and functioning in their off-seasons, before and after bloom, and they must have good growing and living conditions year-round. And that means a healthy bed in well-prepared soil. Soil preparation is the most important cultural element for perennial plants. It affects their access to oxygen and water and the availability of basic plant foods, and it is also a key factor in reliable winter hardiness.

Soil preparation is the most important element for a successful garden.

The Secret Ingredient

It's the rare garden that has soft and loamy organic soil growing plants of bionic proportions, and it's almost never your own. More likely than not, your soil type will fall within the broad categories of rock-hard heavy clay or infertile sandy soil that won't hold water or nutrients. Some gardens have patches of more than one soil type, and those areas will need to be treated differently. But what's missing from both categories is the single most important soil ingredient for healthy plants, and that is humus.

All organic materials compost down to humus, which is the fibrous end product of decomposition. A pile of leaves left on the ground sinks lower and lower as it decomposes, until finally, all that's left is humus, a thin brown layer of vegetable fiber that remains in the soil for many decades. A forest is made lush by many tons of leaves composting down to humus each year and adding to the accumulation of organic fiber in the soil. Small garden compost bins and huge municipal leaf piles produce the same kind and basic quality of humus.

Humus is the life-support system of soil, forming a web-like structure of vegetable fiber that gives soil a spongy soft texture. It holds soil together in a cohesive mass, full of minerals in tiny particles of sand, silt and clay; fragments of organic debris (like leaves, stems and plant parts); and spaces between for the movement of air and water. Humus creates a friendly home environment for the soil microorganisms that process mineral nutrients into plant foods. It promotes the life of ants and ground beetles that feed on insect larvae, as well as beneficial nematodes that parasitize white grubs in lawns. The more humus that is present in garden soil, the fewer insect and disease problems for the gardener.

Every bit of organic material that is added to your soil is digested by worms and microbes, which release nutrients to plants and leave a small deposit of humus. This is like banking gold under your feet, for each bit of humus adds to soil value in a permanent way. Humus in soil works like gluten in bread, spreading a web structure throughout the mass and giving it shape, form and texture. Without enough humus, the small particles of clay soil collapse and compact, trapping water within or keeping it out. Humus helps to separate the dense soil

Humus
The fibrous end product
of decomposition.
=

| Sand, Silt and Clay | + | leaves, stems and plant parts | + | space for air and water |

Humus is made by allowing organic material to decompose in the soil.

If you make your own garden compost, the finished product is rich in natural humus.

Composted leaves and can be an important source of humus in your garden.

particles, open up pathways for water to drain and create air spaces for oxygen.

Conversely, without adequate humus, the large particles of sandy soil fall apart and rapidly drain water and nutrients away from plant roots. Humus binds the sandy particles together, forming a structure to hold water and nutrients in the root zone.

Humus is made in the easiest possible way—by allowing organic material to decompose in the soil. Organic mulch such as shredded leaves or shredded bark that is spread over the soil surface decomposes more slowly but also turns into humus. Instead of sweeping up every last leaf in autumn, allow half of them to remain on areas of bare soil in planting beds, spread over the roots of trees and gathered around the bases of shrubs. One inch (2.5 cm) of shredded leaves spread over the lawn will settle between the blades and improve the soil below. In time, with the assistance of earthworms and an army of soil microbes, the leaves will be processed into finished humus. It's a silent, economical and efficient process of acquiring something of great value and with no cost to the gardener.

If you make your own garden compost, the finished product is rich in natural humus. Peat moss and rotted manure sold in bags are also good sources of humus if you would like to spend some money. But the best humus is made from plant parts found in the garden, and that is mostly tree leaves. Composted leaves are called leaf mold and are an important source of humus. The leaves can be your own or a collection of bagged autumn leaves from neighbors. Dig them in or use them as organic mulch on exposed soil, with the sure knowledge that each leaf is like money in your soil bank.

Soil Check

Recognizing soil types is the key to identifying what kind of soil you've got and, most important, how to change and improve it. Some of you may have heard about soil with good "friability," but do you really know what friable soil looks and feels like? That elusive friability has to do with the physical properties of soil structure. Friable soil is wet but not soaked. It should have the moisture of a squeezed-out sponge. It will hold its shape when

Soil Chemistry

Soil chemistry is not mysterious, but it is complex. Every soil has a level of acidity and alkalinity that can be measured on the pH scale, which runs from 0 to 14. The scale is an indication of the concentration of hydrogen ions that are associated with available soil fertility (think of pH as meaning parts hydrogen). The middle point, pH 7.0, is a neutral level. Values below 7.0 are acidic, and values above the neutral point are alkaline.

The ideal point for most plant growth is between pH 6.3 and pH 6.8, or a slightly acidic reading of a soil sample. At this level, nutrients are freely available, soil animals are most active, and fertility is high. Most plants have difficulty absorbing nutrients when the soil is either strongly acidic (below pH 5.0) or strongly alkaline (above pH 8.0). Plants like rhododendrons, azaleas and heather, which perform best in acidic soil of about pH 5.5 or lower, are exceptions.

What causes a soil to be either acid or alkaline? Gardens over limestone bedrock have alkaline soil; gardens over granite bedrock are more likely to have acidic soil. Moisture also has an influence—dry soil tends toward alkalinity, and wet soils are more acidic.

Additions of limestone or sulfur, both organic elements, can moderate pH. Adding calcitic or dolomitic limestone raises the pH of an acidic soil to a more acceptable level, whereas sulfur lowers the pH of a strongly alkaline soil. But these manipulations are effective for a very short time, perhaps less than one growing season, and the soil quickly returns to its true pH value.

Organic plant material is the only soil constituent with any significant and lasting effect on pH. Humus buffers acidity and alkalinity, and its presence in quantity is directly commensurate with the ability of plants to adapt to soil pH outside their ideal range. The most effective way for gardeners to achieve the best soil possible is to add generous amounts of organic mulch materials each year.

ACIDIC	NEUTRAL	ALKALINE

0	1	2	3	4	5	6	7	8	9	10	11	12	13	14
	Battery Acid	Lemon Juice		Wine		Normal Rain	Distilled Water		Baking Soda	Soft Soap		Ammonia		Lye

compressed in your hand, but gentle pressure from a finger will shatter it. When you spread it across your palm, you feel and see small fragments of leaves and roots, gritty bits of sand and crumbs of dark soil called "peds." It has a sweet and light fragrance that is the hallmark of organic life. When you dig a hole in friable loam, the soil falls away without sticking to the spade. Once you learn to recognize the characteristics of friability, it's easy to understand the shortcomings of your own soil and how to change it for the better. Knowing your soil type and how to renovate it for better plant growth are the keys to easy and successful gardening with perennial plants.

Do you have clay soil?

Just watching how soil behaves can tell you something about its character. Some gardens become temporary lakes for a few weeks in spring as snowmelt water slowly drains away. The "lake effect" is a good indication of slow-draining heavy clay soil, just as puddles in the lawn after a summer downpour are sure indications that the soil beneath is compacted clay. There are several kinds of clay soil, some bluish or mustard in color and others just a dull brown. But what they all have in common is a dense, hard texture that plant roots have difficulty penetrating.

If you must jump on the edge of your spade to get it into the ground, you're digging clay soil. If clods of sticky soil cling to your shovel, you have the stuff from which pottery is made. Take a wet lump and roll it into a sausage shape between your hands. If you roll it on a flat surface, the sausage of clay can be extended into a long string or ribbon. The longer you can extend the ribbon, the greater the percentage of clay in your soil. The sticky plasticity that allows clay to form a ribbon in your hand will compact into a solid mass of dense garden soil. If the clay is in dry condition, the clods may be more like rocks that you can't break apart with your hands.

When clay is wet, water has trouble finding drainage routes and oxygen has difficulty entering the root zone, conditions that cause plants to die from asphyxiation. If the clay is dry, its hardness is impenetrable to moisture and plants die from water starvation. Either way, you won't have a successful perennial garden

> Knowing your soil type and how to renovate it for better plant growth are the keys to easy and successful gardening with perennial plants.

Soil Profiles

Most garden soils can be described as either clay-like or sandy. But within those two descriptions are several categories that better characterize each soil profile. Here are some of the most common:

Sand: Primarily large particles of sand, with a small amount of organic debris.

Loamy sand: A roughly even blend of sand, clay particles, fine silt and organic debris.

Sandy loam: More than half dark soil (clay, silt and organic debris) with at least 25 percent sand.

Loam: Moderately coarse mix of dark soil, with 20 percent organic debris and less than 5 percent sand.

Clay loam: Heavy-textured dark soil, with less than 20 percent organic debris and minimal sand.

Silty clay: Dense brown or gray clay with smooth texture and less than 15 percent sand or organic debris.

Clay: Brown, beige or blue rough-textured clay with less than 10 percent sand or organic debris.

Sandy loam

Sand

Clay loam

Clay

Triple Mix or Topsoil
consists of

LOAM   MANURE   PEAT MOSS

We seldom realize that clay is rich with plant nutrients that come from minerals.

in heavy clay soil. Some gardeners replace large volumes of their clay soil with purchased topsoil or triple mix (loam mixed with peat moss and aged manure). That's a pragmatic solution, and it will give a quick start on planting. But soil is real estate, and you've already paid for it once. It's always a shame to discard a natural resource, even if your clay soil seems completely useless. You might consider how the clay can be amended and renovated and its texture made more workable.

But let's not be too hard on clay—the value of clay soil is often overlooked. We're quick to recognize its deficiencies—too heavy, too hard to dig, constantly wet or chronically dry. But we seldom realize that it is rich with plant nutrients that come from minerals. The dense texture of clay ties up mineral nutrients and makes them inaccessible to plant roots, but they can be unlocked by changing the texture of the clay soil. Amending clay to give it a softer and more open texture is what's required to make nutrients, oxygen and moisture available. It may not be necessary to replace your clay soil in planting areas, especially if you can do some basic work to reform its character.

Changing the texture of clay isn't complicated. Two crucial elements need to be incorporated into the soil—organic material and coarse sand. Organic material, the most important amendment, could be a combination of homemade compost, aged manure, tree leaves and grass clippings. These plant-based materials will bring biological life to the soil, helping to release the clay's mineral nutrients. Adding coarse sand immediately softens the texture of the soil, breaking up the clods of clay and

Leaves, coarse sand and manure help soften the texture of clay, allowing air and water to pass through.

Sources of Organic Material

✓ tree leaves and stems (whole, chopped or shredded)

✓ plant prunings, chopped leaves and stems

✓ weeds (remove roots and flower heads)

✓ grass clippings (unsprayed)

✓ composted sawdust from untreated wood

✓ mushroom compost

✓ aged manure

✓ peat moss

✓ pine needles

✓ cocoa hulls

✓ straw

✓ shredded black newsprint (no colored sections)

establishing spaces for water, oxygen and plant roots to enter. The amounts of organic material and coarse sand should be generous—you really can't add too much—and they need to be dug through the top 18 inches (45 cm) of soil.

This is hard work, but if you do a thorough job and add generous amounts of soil amendments, you won't have to do it again. Plants can be set into the renovated soil right away, and you'll have the quick gratification of seeing them take immediate hold and put on a growth spurt. In subsequent seasons, you can continue to improve the quality of clay soil by adding organic material and coarse sand to every planting hole, but you won't need to do "the big dig" again.

Do you have sandy soil?

Gardens with sandy soil can frustrate your efforts to make anything grow. Their chronic dryness is death to plant roots, and pouring on water is about as effective as pouring it down a drain. There just aren't enough sticky particles of clay and bits of organic plant debris to hold the sand together and "sponge up"

Improving Your Soil

Whenever you plant, try to improve the soil in the planting holes and the immediate area. If the soil quality is poor, remove it and replace with purchased triple mix (a mix of compost, peat moss and loam).

If snowmelt and rain are slow to drain away, improve drainage by digging a little deeper and placing a layer of gravel at the bottom of the planting hole. For shrubs, dig out an additional 10 inches (25 cm) of soil depth and replace it with gravel, then proceed with setting the shrub in place and backfilling with improved soil. For perennial plantings, incorporate coarse builder's sand (not play sand) into the soil in the hole surrounding the roots.

The lion's share of digging takes place in your first year or two of gardening. Make a commitment to improve the soil everywhere you install plants. The most important materials for soil amendment are coarse builder's sand, which improves the amount of oxygen that penetrates into the root zone, and any form of plant leaves you can incorporate into the soil. These two materials will begin to improve drainage, allow the efficient exchange of oxygen and carbon dioxide and soften soil texture to encourage quick root growth.

In the following years, soil improvement becomes easier.

To harness the power of worms and soil microbes, simply lay down thick layers of leaves. Leaves are the natural food source for soil dwellers, and they will repay your generosity by tunneling through soil and enriching it with minerals and fiber. Gather enough leaves in fall to put down a 2-to-3-inch-thick (5–7.5 cm) layer of mulch on all exposed soil around plant crowns. The leaves compress over the winter and then compost over the summer, dissolving into the soil as they are consumed by worms and microbes. A thick layer of leaves provides the added benefit of natural weed suppression.

some of the moisture.

Typically, plants that adapt to sandy soils, such as lavender (*Lavandula angustifolia*) and lamb's ears (*Stachys byzantina*), have fleshy leaves covered with fine hairs that help to conserve moisture within the leaf tissue. They've evolved in hot, sandy regions and seem to know that precious little moisture will be available in the soil.

Although efficient drainage is usually an advantage, sandy soils have too much of a good thing. And if that isn't bad enough, they're also cursed with low fertility because of the absence of organic material and biological life. No one wants these problems. But take heart, for although the circumstances may seem desperate, they are also easily remedied. Easy digging is the one great advantage of sandy soil. And dig you must, adding organic material in geological proportions. Garden compost, aged manure,

peat moss, leaves, lawn clippings, composted sawdust and even shredded newsprint (black ink only, no colored sections) can all be turned under the top 18 inches (45 cm) of soil. Be as generous as possible, for you cannot add too much.

When your digging is done and the sandy soil is thoroughly amended with moisture-holding organic materials, cover the surface of all exposed soil areas with a 2-to-3-inch (5–8 cm) mulch of shredded bark. Plants can be set into the soil by pulling back the mulch to make a hole. Each time you install a plant, make sure you incorporate organic materials like peat moss and aged manure into the hole. The shredded bark mulch will decompose in place and add to the organic content of the soil, saving you from further digging ventures. You'll be surprised at how efficiently the soil "consumes" the mulch, so plan to replace or top it up each year. This process of feeding the soil from the surface works well to conserve and hold moisture around plant roots and stimulate fertility. Combined with a regular irrigation schedule, you might find yourself in a beautiful garden—and it could be your own!

Shredded bark purchased from a garden center is the ideal material for a protective mulch over soil, and it can be applied at any time. But if you require large amounts of mulch, using fallen autumn leaves is more economical and degrades into fiber and soil nutrients.

Planning & Creating Garden Beds

DECIDING WHERE PLANTS WILL BE USEFUL AND HOW THEY can help to define your property is the first important step in establishing a garden. To a new homeowner, plants are practical and affordable tools that can stake out your property in a way that is visible to your neighbors and the public at large. They are also the quickest means to enhance the appearance of a new house on what might still be an unfinished street. Even so, individual plants can't simply be dug into the ground. First, we have to create a home for them, a place where they will thrive and flourish. But how does a new owner go about making the decisions about where these beds should be placed? And how does one go about digging one?

In this chapter, we describe the function of foundation, shrub and perennial beds in your yard. We offer suggestions about the shapes these beds can take and practical ideas on how to get started, as well as an annotated list of recommended plants—but first, a rudimentary list of gardening tools you'll find you can't do without.

Tools

Good tools take the strain off muscles and accomplish the job quickly and efficiently. What's important is that the tool be

> Individual plants can't simply be dug into the ground. First, we have to create a home for them, a place where they will thrive and flourish.

the right size for the job and that it be kept in good condition. Attempting to cut a 2-inch (5 cm) woody branch with hand secateurs (pruners) will likely hurt your hand, break the pruning blade and cause unnecessary damage to the plant. Using a large lopper or pruning saw will remove the branch in minutes, with no stress to the gardener.

Expensive stainless steel shovels look nice hanging from a peg in the garage, but they can't be sharpened, which limits their long-term usability. The best buys in digging tools are moderately priced and available at hardware stores and garden centers. Shovels and spades should be made from metals that can be sharpened with a flint stone. Worth spending serious money for are cutting tools like pruners, loppers and pruning saws with replaceable blades. With thoughtful care, your tools will perform for many years; although if you use them incorrectly, and that includes using them for a job other than the one they were designed to do, you will certainly (and quickly) ruin them. If you attempt to cut a large branch with small pruning shears rather than a large lopper, the blades will be unable to accommodate the girth of the branch and they may even become stuck or wedged in. Our first reaction is to press sideways in an attempt to loosen the shears, but blades and saws are designed only for straight-line forward and backward motions—sideways movements will surely damage them. Always use the right tool for the job at hand.

The Foundation Bed

No matter how lovely it is, without a foundation planting, your new house risks looking like it has fallen off the back of a truck. When filled with attractive plants, a foundation bed—installed on the strip of ground closest to the house walls—helps to gracefully connect the building to the lot. It should stretch along the front façade and perhaps also carry on around a section of the sides of the house if they are highly visible. Be sure to begin digging the bed just beyond the outside edge of the roof eaves, and place plants so that they are away from the wall and have open sky above. Soil directly under the overhang is shaded and chronically dry, so cover this area with a strip of landscape cloth topped with gravel to make it a no-maintenance space.

Caring for Your Tools

Don't leave tools outside overnight where they may be soaked by rain or dew. Use a wire brush to remove clinging soil, and store them in a dry place. Clean them thoroughly at the end of the gardening season, rubbing small spots of rust with sand, and brush the blades lightly with mineral oil to protect the metal surface.

The foundation planting is viewed every day of the year, and should always have a neat presentation. Using precast landscaping pavers to make a mowing strip between the bed and lawn insures the grass edge is never ragged or messy.

Ten Critical Tools

Extraordinary strength isn't required for garden chores. Tools do the work for us, providing we choose the right tool for the right job. Digging a shallow hole for a large perennial clump is quick and easy using a sharp blunt-nosed spade. But the same work is more difficult with a larger shovel, which is hard to maneuver in a small space. Excavating a larger and deeper hole for a heavy shrub requires a long-handled shovel that carries the weight of soil and shift stress away from your back. Digging the same hole with a small spade puts the burden of lift and weight onto your own muscles.

Using tools in scale with the work to be accomplished also applies to small hand tools. Always select pruners, trowels and saws that fit your hand comfortably.

BLUNT-NOSED SPADE for edging beds, planting shrubs and dividing perennials.

LONG-HANDLED SHOVEL for digging heavy soil.

GARDEN FORK for mixing, aerating and turning soil.

STIFF RAKE for spreading soil and organic materials and grading beds and lawns.

Use evergreens with upright conical or pyramidal forms to frame a doorway or fill a blank wall space.

The bed should be a minimum of 5 feet (1.5 m) deep, and preferably closer to 8 feet (2.5 m). It needn't have a straight front line. In fact, a slightly curving line is more elegant. Even just a swelling out of the bed on either side of the front door to accommodate one or two specimen shrubs like weeping white pine (*Pinus strobus* 'Pendula') or dwarf Alberta spruce (*Picea glauca* 'Conica') is sufficient to offset an otherwise straight front line across the front.

Since you'll see your foundation planting almost every day of the year, why not make sure it's attractive in all four seasons? Selecting mostly dwarf evergreens for the front of your home makes the foundation bed attractive even in winter. Use evergreens with upright conical or pyramidal forms to frame a doorway or fill a blank wall space and shorter rounded and mound-shaped evergreens for planting under windows. Take advantage of coniferous plants in various colors and textures to build interest into the arrangement. Seasonal flowering perennials and summer annuals can be tucked between and in front

SOFT RAKE
for gathering
leaves.

**WIDE-BLADE
TROWEL**
for planting
small perennials
and annuals.

**NARROW-BLADE
TROWEL**
for planting
bulbs and re-
moving weeds.

**FOLDING
PRUNING SAW**
for removing
heavy rose canes
and thick shrub
branches.

**BYPASS
PRUNERS**
(also called
secateurs) for
trimming shrubs
and roses.

WHEELBARROW
for moving soil,
rocks and plants
and mixing
organic amend-
ments.

Seasonal flowering perennials and summer annuals can be tucked between and in front of conifers to bring softening effects during the warm months. Plants like perennial geraniums, black-eyed Susan, begonias and impatiens provide plenty of colorful petals from spring through fall. A colorful blooming tree like dwarf magnolia or dwarf crab apple (both of which are available as specimens below 20 feet/6 m) can be set at the house corner farthest from the front door.

Making Garden Beds

Once you've established the location, depth and shape of your ornamental beds, it's time to think about how to create the beds themselves, what materials will be needed and how much work is involved. If there is grass sod over the area selected for a growing bed, it will have to be removed. An effective method is to rent a power sod stripper that slides a bar under the lawn and allows

To keep everything in scale, look for dwarf versions of larger garden specimens for the front of the house.

Plant Height

Tall Plants

Keep plants in scale with the height of doors and windows. Plants that grow so tall and wide that your windows are obscured and entrances squeezed to a narrow access won't complement your home and will be troublesome maintenance problems. Always check the potential size of plants, and look for dwarf versions of larger garden specimens. For example, the *Thuja* 'Green Giant' cedar (42 feet/13 m) works best as a hedge or screen, but dwarf *T. occidentalis* 'Holmstrup' cedar (8 feet/2.5 m)

To keep everything in scale, look for dwarf versions of larger garden specimens for the front of the house.

is perfectly suited for framing a front door entrance. A moderately sized, well-behaved plant is much easier to live with and requires little maintenance.

Other tall plants to consider planting in front of blank walls and to frame doorway entrances include the 'Blue Heaven' juniper (*Juniperus scopulorum* 'Blue Heaven'), a neat pyramidal shrub foliage that needs full sun; the pyramidal Japanese yew (*Taxus cuspidata* 'Capitata'), which likes sun to part shade and has an

upright conical form and dense, dark green foliage; 'DeGroot's Spire' cedar (*Thuja occidentalis* 'DeGroot's Spire'), which likes part shade to sun and has tight green foliage and a narrow columnar form; and two pyramidal cedars that both like part shade to sun: 'Holmstrup' cedar (*T. occidentalis* 'Holmstrup'), with bright green foliage, and 'Sunkist' cedar (*T. occidentalis* 'Sunkist'), with golden-yellow foliage that darkens in winter.

An effective method is to rent a power sod stripper that slides a bar under the lawn and allows grass to be removed in strips.

Short Plants

Low plants to consider include the boxwoods *Buxus* 'Green Velvet' and *B.* 'Green Mountain,' which have small, glossy green leaves and like sun to shade; a handful of variegated euonymus hybirds that have irregular spreading mound shapes and dark green foliage with bold splashes of banding of bright gold: Blondy 'Interbolwi,' 'Golden Prince,' 'Sunspot' and 'Surespot'; the sun-loving compact Mint Julep juniper (*J. chinensis* 'Monlep'), with its mint-green foliage and upward arching branches; and the dwarf Oregon grape (*Mahonia aquifolium* 'Compacta'), which has holly-like foliage, showy yellow spring flowers and likes sun to part shade.

grass to be removed in strips. The strips of grass can be carefully rolled up and used again if you have another area that requires sod (be sure to cover the rolled sod with a sheet of plastic to prevent the exposed roots from drying out, spray lightly with a hose to keep the sod damp, and don't delay the reinstallation longer than a few days).

Digging sod out by hand with a shovel is hard work and can result in the unnecessary loss of soil, which inevitably clings to large clumps of grass. If you're going to remove sod with a handheld tool, use a blunt-nosed shovel with a straight forward edge (not a pointed nose), lay it almost horizontal on the lawn, then dip down and slide it under a section of grass. Press the shovel forward and continue to slide it under the grass, and then lift the grass off in strips. This is slow going, but it will work, and the lifted grass can be used to patch other areas.

Finding a new home for excess sod is sometimes a challenge. If your relatively new lawn doesn't have any rough areas that need patching, lifted sod can be removed to a municipal composting site. Most municipalities have composting yards where old Christmas trees and other garden waste are accepted. If your

Small architectural features add year-round interest to any garden.

How Much Soil Do You Need?

To calculate how much soil you need to create a specific bed, measure the bed's area, estimating the length and width if it is an irregular shape. Multiply its length in feet by the width in feet. Multiply that number by the desired number of inches in depth of new purchased soil, sand or organic amendments. Divide the result by 324. The answer will tell you how many cubic yards of the material need to be ordered.

Length in feet x width in feet x depth of new material in inches. Divide by 324.
Answer is in cubic yards.

(Metric formula: Length in meters x width in meters x depth of new material in centimeters. Divide by 100. Answer is in cubic meters.)

front or back yards have any areas that are depressed or sunken, the sod can be used to fill in and raise the grade level. Lay the sod in the depression green side down, with the root side upward, and pack it down with some additional topsoil. The buried sod will compost, turning to soil that will help to raise the grade.

When it comes to your soil, it's important to get an early sense of what you're dealing with. You may have to work hard to augment it (see "Soil Basics," page 18), perhaps with soil ordered from a garden center or another supplier.

Soil quality is key to plant growth, and every category of soil benefits from organic amendments such as leaves, composted animal manures, pine needles and peat moss. Purchased peat moss is a beautiful material, but it is often finely milled and quickly disappears into soil. Peat is good for individual planting holes and small areas, but larger beds (like a vegetable plot) benefit from generous amounts of leaves and manure. Small leaves (like birch, locust, apple, beech and some oaks), as well as shredded large leaves from maples, are excellent materials to incorporate into soil. Soil organisms cause them to slowly decompose and to contribute mineral plant foods and humus fiber that holds

moisture in the root zone and conditions the soil.

Dense soil may hold too much water and not enough oxygen to support plant life, a problem that can be solved by digging in coarse builder's sand or one-quarter-inch (0.6 cm) gravel, breaking up clay and creating pore spaces for water to drain and oxygen to enter the soil. If this is your problem, plan on spreading a 3-inch (7.5 cm) depth of sand or gravel over the areas and digging it in to a depth of at least 12 inches (30 cm).

Stripping the sod of a new suburban lawn may well reveal an inch or two (2.5–5 cm) of topsoil that has been spread over an inhospitable bed of gravel and rocks. It might also expose soil that is more like compacted blue or beige clay. A decision needs to be made about the possible rehabilitation of this inferior soil. Can it be done, or is it better to excavate the bed areas and replace them with purchased premium soil? Both methods involve considerable labor and some expense.

It's always preferable to amend the soil, adding materials that will improve texture, fertility and drainage. Dig a test hole and see what you come up with. If the soil is littered with small rocks and gravel, they can be useful to establish good drainage, providing they make up no more than 20 percent of the soil mass. Consider the color of soil you excavate. Any shade of brown indicates that some amount of organic material is present, and this soil can be improved by adding more organic materials. If the soil has a

Introducing sand lightens compacted dense soil, allowing water to drain and oxygen to reach plant roots.

If the soil is littered with small rocks and gravel, they can be useful to establish good drainage, providing they make up no more than 20 percent of the soil mass.

waxy blue sheen or is compacted beige hardpan clay, those are soils that should be replaced.

If you decide that the soil in your planting beds must be replaced, expect to move quite a volume of soil out of the holes. To give new plants a good root run and also allow enough depth for drainage, replace a depth of 18 to 24 inches (45–60 cm) of soil in the bed. Getting rid of the soil can be a problem, but there may be an inventive use for it on your property. Excess soil is often used to construct a berm in the garden—a small hill or rise in grade, used to bring interest to an otherwise flat landscape. It can be covered with a layer of good topsoil and planted with grass. Otherwise, for a fee, a building contractor may accept the unwanted soil for disposal.

When ordering soil for planting beds, try to find a supplier who sells clean topsoil, free from wood debris and weed seeds. Garden centers can refer you to a soil supplier or may be able to supply it themselves. If you order topsoil, a kind of heavy loam that is taken from the top 2 inches (5 cm) of soil, it should be dark, sweet-smelling and not too heavy. Squeeze a handful to firm it into a ball, then tap it with your finger and see if it shatters. If the clod remains intact, there's probably too much clay in the mix and it will be tough on plant roots. If topsoil fits comfortably into your budget, you can certainly amend it with leaves as you fill the beds, which will improve and lighten the texture. Another choice is triple mix, a more expensive soil product made up of topsoil enriched with compost and peat moss. Triple mix is a soft, friable and nutritionally rich mix that is premium grade for planting beds.

Remember that it is impractical to purchase bagged soil to fill excavated garden beds. Bulk loads of soil are purchased in cubic yards, and the delivery arrives in a truck. The driver expects to drop the soil in your driveway or at the edge of the curb, and you're responsible for moving it by wheelbarrow to where it's needed. If the soil can't be immediately moved or if the work won't be finished in the same day, be sure to cover the pile with a tarp weighted down by bricks to prevent wind and rain from eroding it and making a mess of the street.

Not everyone has the strength (or willing helpers with strong

Be sure to cover the pile of soil with a tarp weighted down by bricks to prevent wind and rain from eroding it.

muscles) to dig out garden beds. In that case, it's possible to establish the bed over existing lawn if you start in very early spring, allowing enough time before planting season begins. Cover the area with a six-page thickness of black and white newsprint (no colored sections because of the chemicals in colored dyes). On top of this layer, heap purchased triple mix or loamy topsoil purchased in cubic yards from a soil supplier. To accommodate the growth of perennial plants, you'll need to heap the purchased soil to approximately 20 to 24 inches (50–60 cm) high, and then wet it down with a hose (but don't saturate the soil or it will run off). This will look like a huge amount of soil, but over four weeks, it will sink to half the height.

Remember that what you're creating is effectively a raised bed, and it must contain enough soil, at least 12 inches (30 cm) in height, to prevent frost damage to plant roots. The heaped soil is ready for planting in two to three weeks, after most of the sinking has taken place. Exposed soil around plants in the bed should

A raised bed can be created on top of existing grass, eliminating the hard work of digging out garden beds.

A raised bed must contain enough soil, at least 12 inches (30 cm) in height, to prevent frost damage to plant roots.

be covered with 2 to 3 inches (5–7.5 cm) of an organic mulch that is made with leaves or shredded bark purchased from a garden center. Small-sized bark chips are also good mulching material; avoid the larger chips that tend to dry out and move around. Trim any exposed edges of newsprint, and using a blunt-nosed shovel or half-moon edging tool, cut a sharp, deep defining edge to the bed all around.

Planting Beds

With the house foundation, the perimeter lines and the lawn tree issues decided, now it's time to consider planting beds that will be focal points of seasonal bloom. Planting beds can be set around the garden perimeter, backing onto fences or hedges, set as informal planting areas amidst shrub borders or freestanding as island beds in a lawn. It's important that the beds are visible for the full blooming season. (If your yard is large or has an unusual shape, it may be that some beds are out of sight from the house, and that will add to their interest as you must travel out a bit to see what's going on there.)

When deciding on the shape of your beds, keep in mind that a traditional rectangular bed makes a more appealing visual statement if you dress up a corner with a small weeping tree and a cluster of boulders. A corner bed, on the other hand, is dynamic by definition, presenting several planting options within a balanced form. A narrow bed can appear wider with the addition of some graceful scalloping across the front edge, while a kidney-shaped bed lends itself to Victorian displays of bedding plants and tall ferns at the other end. A round bed on its own has a formal look, but if you mound it slightly with additional earth, it becomes more relaxed. A crescent-shaped bed can help to break up large areas and define your lawn.

Close and Distant Locations

Standing first at the front entrance and then at the back door, consider where an ornamental planting bed would be best viewed. Nobody will ever complain about having a beautiful view into the garden from the window over the kitchen sink. A planting bed can follow the partial length along one side of a path, or a

Planting beds can be set around the garden perimeter, backing onto fences or hedges, set as informal planting areas amidst shrub borders or freestanding as island beds in a lawn.

small corner bed can be made where a vertical front yard sidewalk from the street or horizontal path from the driveway intersect, softening the juncture. These are places for a bright burst of summer annuals that are low-growing (under 12 inches/30 cm) with neat clump forms, such as impatiens and fibrous begonias. Large functional areas, like a double driveway, can be brought into the garden plan when one long side is lined with an informal bed of daylilies and black-eyed Susan. If your lawn tree has a slender trunk (such as a Japanese maple or an ornamental pear), you might want a crescent-shaped bed to partially surround and complement the tree. That would be a good place for early- and late-blooming perennial geraniums, spotted deadnettle, hostas and a bright annual such as red or blue salvia.

Deeper into the backyard, the classic perimeter beds can follow one or both sides of the lot and also along the farthest back line. It might make more sense to begin with a perimeter bed on just one side of the garden (you can add another next year), in the area of greatest light or in the location that is most visible from

A deep band of summer annuals will provide consistent color from spring through frost, and is easily changed for a different color scheme each year. The long ribbon planting has the benefit of making a small space appear larger.

Shade-Tolerant Plants

Sweet woodruff

Spotted deadnettle

house windows. You might have different light values in each of these places, so you should consider whether they are suitable for the particular kind of plants you want to grow. If you haven't any special plants in mind, be assured that there are sun-loving and shade-tolerant plants suitable for all but deep shade (and in a new home, you're unlikely to encounter that kind of low light). In a shaded area, you might want only a narrow bed filled with shade-loving ground-cover plants like sweet woodruff (*Galium odorata*), 'White Nancy' spotted deadnettle (*Lamium maculatum*) and green and white 'Jack Frost' Siberian bugloss (*Brunnera macrophylla*). Along a brighter side of the garden, you can make a deeper border with room for many more blossoming perennials.

If you intend to make a planting bed in front of a hedge line, be sure your plants won't crowd and shade the hedge. Leave enough space so that light can fall between the hedge and the ornamental plants in front of it. (You can place several flat patio stones in the space, which will give you a firm surface to stand on when grooming plants.) Plan on making primary ornamental beds 5 to

Siberian bugloss

There are sun-loving and shade-tolerant plants suitable for all but deep shade.

8 feet (1.5–2.5 m) wide, allowing space for plants to form generous clumps (producing more flowers each year) and allowing enough depth so that clumps won't be set out in straight lines. A slightly offset and jumbled plant placement creates a more natural presentation to the full border. If you are enthusiastic about growing ornamental plants, the border could be up to 10 feet (3 m) wide, but beyond that, you should be prepared for serious amounts of maintenance work.

The front edge of any garden bed helps establish your garden's style. A straight edge across the border demonstrates conservative control and a formal attitude. If you want a more gracious and relaxed style, allow the front line to curve slightly, perhaps swelling out at one or both ends. Establishing the front line of the bed is more complicated than it might seem: Don't rush through this important step. Use a rubber garden hose (a vinyl hose won't cooperate with you) to create the line in the grass, then step away and look at it from a distance (even from an upper-story window). You'll probably want to adjust the line and examine it again. You'll be surprised to discover that your feelings about the line can change overnight. It's worth taking a couple of days with this experiment until you've got the line just how you like it. This is time well spent, because it's the most prominent style statement you'll make in the garden.

If your lawn is expansive, you might want to put an island bed in it to break up the space. Island beds typically look best when set slightly off center, a more relaxed placement that suggests it just naturally belongs there. If you set an island bed in the direct center of the lawn, it creates a formal focal point that requires significant enhancement. You'll need a plant or object of substance to anchor the central point, and that could be a specimen weeping shrub or small tree or an architectural piece, like a small fountain, elevated sundial or birdbath.

Planting Primer

You've dug the beds and amended the soil, and now you're ready to plant. But how do you keep your plants happy once they're installed in their new homes? Here are a few things to keep in mind.

When choosing locations for your plants, make sure that the information about light requirements on the garden center tags and your chosen spots are of one mind. Since sunlight provides the ultraviolet rays that are essential to plant growth and flower production, it's often assumed that perennials require as much light as possible. But if that were true, there would be no ferny glades, no shady bowers, no sylvan dells where the cowslips grow.

Plants that have evolved for thousands of years in particular locations, such as woodland or mountain ridge, will develop capabilities to thrive in similar light circumstances. Low shrubs from stony alpine slopes adapt well to sunny hillsides in full sun. Woodland ramblers that grow under tree canopies are at home in a shady urban garden. The strategy is to match the plant with the available light quality, and that means you must understand the light in your garden.

Measuring the light in your garden is easy if the sun shines

The strategy is to match the plant with the available light quality, and that means you must understand the light in your garden.

into every corner all day long. But when trees and structures get in the way for a portion of the day, you have more than one kind of light. Full sun refers to positions that receive six hours or more of direct sunlight each day. Partial shade is sunlight for three to five hours. Less than three hours of direct sunlight might be dappled shade with some sunlight. Bright shade locations receive no direct sunlight but have such an open location that bright light, referred to as sky-shine, is reflected from the sky. And, of course, anything less than this is consistently dimmer and darker.

No Place Like Home

Like people, plants are resistant to change, and it's important to approach these changes with a gentle touch. The simple act of being moved from a pot to the new hole in the soil is stressful for plants. They may experience some shock from having their roots loosened. They sense the difference in temperature from warmer ambient air aboveground to the cooler temperature below ground, and that whole process makes strong demands for water from the root system. Plants require at least 10 hours to adjust to these changes, and that's a hard adjustment to make in bright sunlight. Instead, time your planting for a cloudy day, or wait until direct sunlight leaves the garden, typically toward the end of the afternoon or in early evening.

What's next when providing plant life insurance? Simply put, it's preparing a good hole for each plant, one that is structured to encourage the rapid, strong root development so crucial to winter hardiness. Plants with well-developed root systems are able to manufacture generous amounts of carbohydrate energy used to build the fibers that protect them from deep frost. When root development is slow and limited, however, plants may suffer extensive twig dieback in winter. If you've made a good hole for your plant, you can be reasonably certain it will remain healthy and intact through the winter months.

Plants sold in 4- or 6-inch (10 or 15 cm) pots grow into big clumps within three seasons if they stay healthy. You'll get quicker performance and more flowers by digging the hole twice as deep and three times as wide as the plant's root ball. A perennial in a 4-inch (10 cm) pot should have a hole dug 8 inches (20 cm) deep

and 12 inches (30 cm) wide. Larger pots of purchased perennials can be planted in holes using the same ratio of twice the depth and three times the width.

The ideal planting soil is a mixture of what's taken from the hole combined with organic amendments and coarse sand. (If your soil is already sandy, you need only to add generous amounts of organic ingredients.) Remove the soil from the hole and put half of it in a bucket, spreading the remaining half over another part of the planting area. Mix in similar amounts of organic material and coarse sand (if needed) to equal the original volume. A good enrichment mix for planting holes is four parts peat moss, four parts aged manure, one part blood meal and one part bonemeal. These organic amendments supply nutrients to the plants, while the coarse sand breaks up clay, carries oxygen into the hole and establishes good drainage.

Before you plant, trim off any broken stems and decaying leaves. Remove the plant from its pot by turning it upside down and gently pressing on the bottom and sides until it slides out. Don't pull on leaves or the central stem if the plant resists movement; if necessary, you can soak the entire pot in warm water to loosen the root ball. As you remove each plant, check its root system. When plants have been stranded too long in pots waiting for someone to get them into the ground, their roots can be

A stone house and boulder landscaping require plants to lighten the image. Select trees and shrubs with colorful foliage, incorporating bright green, chartreuse, variegated green and white, and deep burgundy.

tightly compressed against the sides of the pot. If you see roots massed on the outside or if the entire root ball seems like a compressed bundle of roots, slightly loosen the outside surfaces (by digging your fingertips into the root ball) to allow new roots to grow out into the hole. Large thick roots can be gently pulled out; a solid mass of fine fibrous roots can be gently torn to open up the root ball.

Then, put enough of the amended soil mix in the hole to bring the new plant up to ground level, set the plant in the hole, and fill in around it with the soil mix. Gently firm the plant down, but don't compact and press oxygen out of the soil surrounding the root ball.

Cover the root area with mulch, and provide a generous drink of water to settle the plant. Wet the soil throughout the hole. A transplant fertilizer can be mixed into the drink to promote quick root growth. If the plant has wilted visibly, provide temporary shade for a day or two by putting a box or garden chair nearby to block direct sunlight.

Planting for Difficult Situations

Every gardener wants the best growing conditions possible, but all too often, circumstances fall short of ideal. Although poor soil can be amended to improve texture and fertility, environmental factors are hard to control. Intense light and heat, wind exposure in summer and winter, deep shade and soil that is chronically dry or permanently saturated are some of the most difficult conditions for plants.

Too Bright, Hot and Dry

Gardens with full exposure to sunlight as well as dry soil present plants with the greatest challenges, and in summer months, heroic rescue measures are frequently required. Ultraviolet rays can exhaust plant tissues and send leaves into full wilt by midday, when the sun is directly overhead. Water pressure in plant tissues keeps leaves and stems turgid, a term describing the normal erect posture of plant parts. But even with adequate

Clockwise from left: musk mallow, Russian sage, and perennial cornflower are good bets for a hot, dry space.

moisture in the soil, internal hydraulic systems can't pump water fast enough into the slumping upper portions of the plant. Although stems and leaves may return to their normal rigid posture when the sun passes away, repeated wilting diminishes plant performance.

The first defense against extreme heat and sun exposure is an organic soil. Amending the soil with organic materials like compost, aged manure, peat moss and shredded leaves ensures that water is held in the root zone and available when plants need it. Shredded bark mulch 2 to 3 inches (5–7.5 cm) thick covering

The first defense against extreme heat and sun exposure is an organic soil.

exposed soil around plants preserves the water underground. Soil exposed to intense sunlight can heat up enough to cook plant roots, and thick mulch also helps to lower temperature in the root zone.

Selecting plants with drought-hardy characteristics is a smart approach to planting in hot places. Foliage covered with fine hairs that shade the leaf surface, such as perennial cornflower (*Centaurea montana*), are usually prepared to make a good show in a hot site. Plants with deep taproots, like musk mallow (*Malva moschata*), can rely on water stored deeper underground, away from the sunlight. Gray-leafed plants, like Russian sage (*Perovskia atriplicifolia*), evolved in arid regions and want a bright, hot and dry site. Grouping plant clumps in clusters allows them to provide a little shade to the others and also forms a slight microclimate of cooler air inside the cluster. Consider making some shade with the addition of a shrub or small tree on the southwest side of the planting. Even a large rock provides some relief from sun if plants are gathered on the east and north sides.

Of course, a regular irrigation program makes a great difference to the well-being of plants in hot and dry conditions. Even plants with drought-hardy characteristics perform better with regular watering. They may be able to survive on rainwater alone, but if you want them to have an attractive appearance, supplemental watering is key. A brief watering that wets just the top 1 to 2 inches (2.5–5 cm) of soil is inadequate and will mostly be lost to evaporation. Provide water in early morning or early evening when the sun is down. It's important to water long and slowly, allowing moisture to seep deeply into the root zone. A weeper hose is the best way to ensure water goes where it's needed. Put it down for the season, turning it on for several hours in the evening or early part of the day.

Too Much Shade

In a shady garden, you'll need to make the most of what light you have. If your new property features a large, shade-creating tree, call in an arborist to remove the lowest limbs, and have the crown thinned and opened. You may be surprised at how much light is increased by adjusting the trees. But don't do it yourself. Any

A shade garden could include plants with variegated green-and-white foliage that reflect light, like these hostas.

If you have a wet garden, select plants that tolerate this sort of soil, such as the silverleaf dogwood, facing page, or the American elder, above.

Painting fences and trellises a light color of gray or taupe (but not white, which is too bright) helps to reflect available light onto plants.

tree climbing above 10 feet (3 m) is work for a professional with the best equipment and safety precautions. If shade is caused by a neighboring structure, that's a more permanent problem. Painting fences and trellises a light color of gray or taupe (but not white, which is too bright) helps to reflect available light onto plants.

Plants in a shady site are already struggling with low light, and poor soil conditions create a double deprivation. Again, amending the soil generously with organic materials like compost, aged manure, peat moss and leaves ensures that moisture is available in the root zone. If the massive roots of mature trees take all available water, creating dry shade conditions, it may be useful to make mounded or raised beds to elevate shrubs and perennial plants.

A shady garden imposes limits on what can be grown, eliminating the big bloomers like roses, peonies and lilacs. In the biological processes of plants, low light means low energy, and

Your First Garden

Silverleaf dogwood

shady conditions result in fewer flowers and fruits. Plants make energy by combining ultraviolet light and basic nutrients they take from the soil. Fortunately, some plants can adapt to the diminished light and provide generous blossoms and ornamental foliage. Choose shade-tolerant plants, and buy slightly more than you think are necessary. Plants in shade tend to become tall and lankier as they reach for light, and you'll need more to fill the space. Try to include plants with variegated green-and-white foliage that reflect light and brighten the scene.

Too Wet

Of all the problematic planting conditions, excessive water in the soil is by far the worst. When water is trapped in soil, it locks air and oxygen out of the root zone, stunting growth and eventually asphyxiating plants. Normally, water drains out of soil through a system of pores and spaces and is replaced with air. Whether in bright or shady light, the difficulties of water-saturated soil are similar, and so are the solutions. If the soil is dense clay, it's possible to improve the soil texture and, by digging in coarse builder's sand and even a half inch (1 cm) of gravel, to break up the clay and allow water to drain through. Digging in organic materials also helps establish spaces in the soil for the exchange of moisture and air. Select plants that tolerate wet soil, such as red chokeberry (*Aronia arbutifolia*), summersweet (*Clethra alnifolia*), silverleaf dogwood (*Cornus alba*) and American elder (*Sambucus canadensis*).

High Performance in a Low-Maintenance Garden

NEW GARDENERS AND EXPERIENCED GROWERS SHARE one fundamental goal—they want to choose plants that will thrive and beautify the property. Likewise, whether you stay in your new home for just a few years or regard it as a long-term dream come true, careful plant selection and planting techniques will put the best face on your personal landscape and make your effort and investment worthwhile.

Much of gardening is based on experimentation—trying new plants to see how adaptable they are to the growing conditions in your own garden. Inevitably, there are plants that do well and some that fail entirely. Understanding why plants fail can take time, thought and research. But the reward of bounteous blossoms from dependable plants is what keeps gardeners going when more temperamental plants fail to produce. Having a core group of high-performance perennials and flowering shrubs that succeed every year provides beauty, satisfaction and bouquets for extended periods, which frees you up to experiment with other plants.

High-performance perennials can be counted on to return every year and bloom for an extended period, often four to six weeks (perennials with a lower performance pattern may bloom for only three weeks). They might be the plants your parents grew or plants that you admired over the neighbor's fence. But their best

High-performance perennials can be counted on to return every year and bloom for an extended period, often four to six weeks.

characteristic is a dependable and long season of bloom. Decades ago, when fewer varieties of perennials were available, high-performance perennials were all-stars in the garden. Now they're the reliable backbone of planting beds with much broader diversity.

The good news is that there's no end in sight to interesting new perennials. Today, plant nurseries are shipping them across the continent and importing new species and hybrids every growing season, making available a "plant pool" that increases exponentially each year. But while you're waiting for the results on new selections, you can enjoy success with the well-loved and familiar perennials that are low-maintenance and long-blooming.

Similarly, flowering shrubs are plants that deliver ornamental value without demanding a lot of care. They have predictable blooming times that span the seasons from late winter through

Rhododendrons are high performers when they're grown in acidic soil with a pH of 6.0 or less.

Lilacs provide a lavish bloom in the spring but also serve as a reliable garden backbone all year long.

early fall, providing generous flower displays and bringing a variety of textures and forms to the garden. Most of our attention goes to the flower display, and that can be lavish when you consider the potential bloom from plants like lilacs and hydrangeas. But the mature height and width of shrubs are also important parts of the garden's backbone—that is, the living furniture in the garden space. Shrub forms can be upright or spreading and dense or delicately structured, and these differing shapes encourage character and appeal in planted areas. Fortunately, a lot of plant-breeding work has resulted in flowering shrub species suitable for both small and large gardens. Today, there are even dwarf specimens that fit into small spaces where there is limited room for growth.

The Beauty of Low Maintenance

What does "low maintenance" mean? For starters, it doesn't mean no maintenance—unless you want a completely naturalistic garden where native plants roam at will. No matter which plants you've chosen, they will require some degree of attention, and they'll probably need it more than once in a season.

If you're uncertain about how long you'll live in your new house and have limited time, be disciplined in how many plants and growing beds you establish. But if you expect to remain in the house for a decade or longer and have time for regular maintenance, you can begin planning additional garden areas and phase in plant installations over two or three years.

Low-maintenance plants perform well with minimum assistance from the gardener, requiring little more than adequate moisture. They have strong, healthy growth patterns and don't display inherent weaknesses or vulnerabilities. In different habitats, low-maintenance plants are defined by specific criteria, described below.

Soil adaptability

Choose plants that are adaptable to a wide range of soil conditions or plants that flourish in your particular conditions.

Plants that don't have special soil or fertilizer requirements are adaptable to a reasonable range of pH values, from slightly acid to slightly alkaline. Even plants considered not adaptable by this criterion can be deemed low-maintenance when they are planted

in the situations they favor. For example, in areas of North America where the soil is naturally acidic, acid-loving rhododendrons and azaleas would be considered low-maintenance. But when they are grown in regions with alkaline soil, they require special soil renovation and frequent attention. Choose plants that are adaptable to a wide range of soil conditions or plants that flourish in your particular conditions.

Rhododendrons and azaleas need acidic soil, but when conditions are right they are beautiful, low-maintenance plants.

With its strong stem, the tree peony provides height and color without needing to be staked.

Traditional tall delphiniums require staking. Avoid the need for stakes by planting low dwarf delphinium hybrids like 'Blue Mirror,' 'Blue Elf,' and 'Blue Pygmy.'

No staking

Save time by growing plants that don't require staking and tying stems in place. Stems of plants should have enough resilience to bend with the wind and rain and then spring back into place. If you don't want them lying all over the ground, double peonies with top-heavy flowers require staking, but single peonies and woody Japanese tree peonies, which have strong stems with less weight at the top, remain erect. The tallest forms of delphinium can reach 7 feet (2 m) and need to be staked, but shorter varieties, like 4-foot (1.2 m) 'Connecticut Yankee' and 3-foot (1 m) belladonna hybrids (the charming butterfly delphiniums), can look after themselves in the wind.

Pest resistance

The garden should be a healthy environment for plants and people. Nothing is more depressing to a gardener than witnessing the downward spiral of a once-healthy plant now afflicted with unstoppable disease. Spraying with chemical remedies is not the answer. Most plant diseases are natural organisms in the landscape and can't be effectively controlled. The best insurance against disease is a combination of low-maintenance plants with inbred resistance—like many phlox hybrids with resistance to mildew—and good cultural practices and growing conditions. Making sure that there is enough air circulation around your plants prevents more disease than does any form of chemical intervention. Plants chronically troubled by destructive insects should also be avoided. A small amount of insect damage is tolerable, because plants and insects are co-dependent partners in the ecosystem, relying on each other for sustenance and reproduction. Only 10 percent of insects are capable of damaging plants, and the other 90 percent work to protect them. Insect damage tends to come in cycles as bug populations rise and then decrease. But when critters make a complete meal of the hostas, it's time to stop growing hostas for a while, until the cycle of destructive behavior changes for the better. And it will.

Polite root systems and seeds

Vigorous perennials are every gardener's dream. You want to see the robust energy in a plant as it extends the shoots, stems and buds that tell you it's headed for a season of fabulous bloom. But if an invasive root system is also roiling underground, that could lead to a less pleasant, high-maintenance situation. Plants with invasive root systems march forward with determination, colonizing everything in their path. That's why one mint plant becomes a mint meadow before gardeners have even had breakfast. But low-maintenance perennials stay within their clumps, expanding and growing fatter each year and keeping to the original location. When perennials have been in the garden for a few years and have reached maturity, it's not unusual for low-maintenance plants to sow a few of their own seeds. Young seedlings of favorite plants are often welcome surprises and a no-work way to fill the borders and make gifts to friends. But if the plant is producing enough seed to fill a grain silo and every one of them is germinating, that isn't going to be a low-maintenance situation.

To prevent mint from running roots through your garden, plant it first into a container and sink the container into the ground.

Winter hardiness

Selecting perennials with a hardiness zone rating that extends to colder regions beyond your own garden is the best way to avoid having to wrap plants in burlap or another protective material to prevent winter losses. Perennials with a hardiness rating two zones colder than your region are a sure bet to survive winter wind, snow and ice. If you live in USDA Zone 6 (coldest temperatures −10°F/−23°C), select plants that are hardy to USDA Zone 4 (coldest temperatures −30°F/−34°C), and they will undoubtedly survive the winters for many years. Plants that are borderline hardy or at the very edge of their hardiness zone will require extra winter protection to ensure survival, and that's a job you don't want.

Perennials with a hardiness rating two zones colder than your region are a sure bet to survive winter wind, snow and ice.

Extended blooming time

Not every plant is able to produce flowers over a long stretch of time. Some have evolved in cool regions with short growing seasons, and their blossom and seed production sequence is shortened by premature frost conditions. Many perennials put out their flowers over a period of 14 to 21 days, and that's the end of flower production for the season. But others continue making

Making sure that there is enough air circulation around your plants prevents more disease than does any form of chemical intervention.

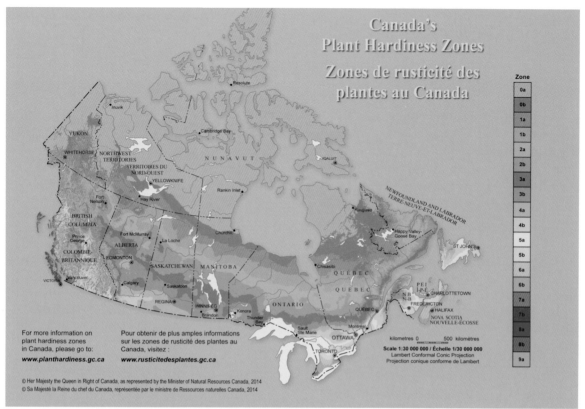

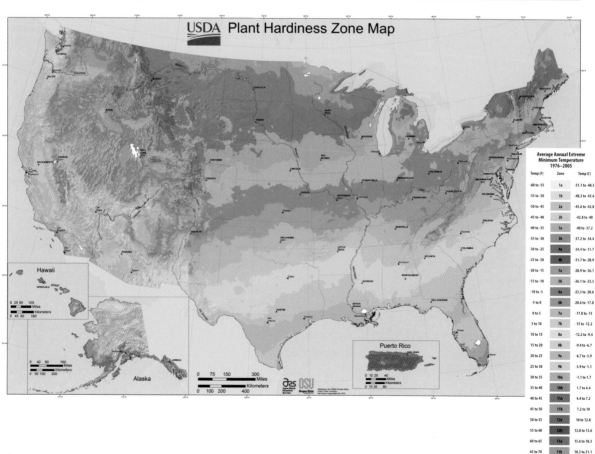

Your First Garden

Basics of Plant Nutrition

Nitrogen
Symbol: N

Nitrogen influences deep green color in leaves and the elongation of stalks and stems. It is essential in the formation of amino acids and proteins, the building blocks of plant growth. Deficiency of nitrogen leads to spindly growth and yellowing foliage. However, excessive nitrogen produces soft tissues with high water content that are prone to fungal diseases and frost damage. Too much nitrogen favors stem and leaf growth at the expense of buds, flowers and fruits. High concentrations of nitrogen can also induce potassium deficiency.

Phosphorus
Symbol: P

Phosphorus is essential to the process of manufacturing carbohydrate plant food during photosynthesis. It plays a strong role in the formation of nucleic acids and other energy-carrying molecules and is important to carbohydrate metabolism and how plants are able to absorb and use nutrients. Phosphorus deficiency results in poor root growth; bluish, bronzed or purple leaves; and poor bud set, ripening and seed set. Phosphorus can be applied to the soil by using bonemeal, which contains a particularly high percentage.

Potassium
Symbol: K

Potassium is the most abundant of the major nutrients in green tissues and is important to plant health and disease prevention. It influences strong cell walls, rigid stems and resilient flowers and fruits. Potassium deficiency causes floppy stems, poor root growth and a characteristic red or purple coloration of the foliage. Growing tips of stems are especially affected, and flower and fruit formation is poor.

flowers for four to six weeks, and those are good candidates for a high-performance garden.

Choosing plants with extended blossoming capability is a good start, but you can make the show last even longer with cultural practices. Perennial plants are driven by a single goal—to produce flowers that will make seeds. Their first flush of flowers is put out with the purpose of maturing seeds for reproduction, and when that objective is accomplished, they settle back into quiet vegetative growth for the remaining days before frost. If you're prepared to meddle a bit in their reproductive process, however, that needn't be the case.

Cutting off, or deadheading, spent flowers before they can form seeds is a simple way to frustrate the plant's objective and trigger a new flush of bloom. The second set of flowers can also be

Plant Hardiness Zone Maps help gardeners select plant species that will grow in the region in which they live.

Fertilizer Basics

Gardeners are anxious parents, eager to provide supplementary nutrients in return for increased blossoms. The key to using organic or manufactured fertilizers effectively is to know when plants can benefit from extra nutrients and how much to apply. Almost every gardener has made mistakes with fertilizers, perhaps using them at the wrong time and causing winter injury or by providing too much fertilizer and burning plant roots. The basic nutrients (nitrogen, phosphorus and potassium) contained in healthy soil are sufficient for the daily maintenance of plant growth. Fertilizers used in moderation increase plant size and number of blossoms, if they are applied at the right time.

Plants have their own growth schedule to carry them through each growing season, and the time to apply fertilizers is when new growth is evident in spring and early summer. It's crucial to wait for plants to initiate their own new growth first, so watch for breaking buds, lengthening shoots and expanding plant clumps and crowns. Trying to rush plants by providing fertilizer before new growth is obvious endangers their performance and life span. Plants begin to grow in response to rising spring soil and air temperatures that trigger growth hormones. Trying to force the trigger with an early jolt of supplemental nutrients is like driving a car with the emergency brake on. You might be able to move it forward, but there will be damage.

Fertilizers can safely be applied in May, just after plants initiate growth, and then again six weeks later. Applying fertilizers after the end of July interferes with the process of maturing and hardening new root and crown tissue and forces tender growth that will be vulnerable to winter damage. Whatever form of fertilizer you select, whether organic or manufactured, pay careful attention to the numbers on the package. They represent the percentage of the three major nutrients contained in the package. If the numbers (sometimes referred to as the analysis) are 8-12-3, the fertilizer is 8 percent nitrogen, 12 percent phosphorus and 3 percent potassium. The remaining 77 percent of the contents in a dry granular fertilizer is a filler or carrier for the nutrients.

Water-soluble fertilizer crystals are easy to mix and apply, but plants absorb relatively little of the nutrients—possibly as low as 10 percent—and the larger part of the mixture runs away from the root zone. If you gently

Trying to rush plants by providing fertilizer before new growth is obvious endangers their performance and life span.

Easy as 1-2-3

The main plant nutrients are nitrogen for deep green color and strong leaf growth; phosphorus for aggressive root development and bud set; and potassium for healthy tissues. Every fertilizer bag or box has three numbers on it representing the amounts of the basic nutrients contained, and they are always listed in the order of nitrogen, phosphorus and potassium. If the numbers are 10-15-6, it means the fertilizer is 10 percent (by weight) nitrogen, 15 percent phosphorus and 6 percent potassium. (A carrier for the nutrients makes up a large portion of the fertilizer weight.)

All numbers of a basic fertilizer for ornamental garden plants should be below 20. Anything higher and you run the risk of damaging the plants.

Before fertilizing, watch for signs of breaking buds, lengthening shoots and expanding plant clumps and crowns as seen here with this hosta in spring.

Fertilizer can be applied in liquid or granular form. Granular fertilizer is longest acting when it is a slow-release encapsulated product that is more expensive, but has extended value.

mix dry granular fertilizers into the soil surrounding the plant with a trowel or hand fork (this involves a bit more effort and time than applying liquid), the fertilizer will stay in the root zone longer, as nutrients are leached out by soil moisture.

Fertilizers with higher numbers in the analysis are more expensive to purchase, and the price reflects the larger volume of nutrient products contained in the package. But this isn't a time to splurge on a rich meal. Plants can be seriously overfed, sometimes with disastrous results, when repeatedly given fertilizers with high numbers like 20-20-20. High amounts of nitrogen can burn plant roots, setting back spring growth and sacrificing potential bloom. And when fed such a rich amount of nutrients, plants are forced to interrupt essential biological sequences, such as seed production and disease resistance, and direct all energy toward rapid growth. If you have already purchased a fertilizer with a high number analysis, use it sparingly at half the recommended rate.

Perhaps the most convincing reason for being conservative with supplemental nutrients is that excessive nitrogen develops soft green tissue with lowered disease resistance and encourages the growth of leaves and stems—all at the expense of buds and flowers. The desire for the maximum number of flowers from each plant is reason enough to use fertilizers with low numbers, all below 20. Garden greed is sometimes a useful instinct.

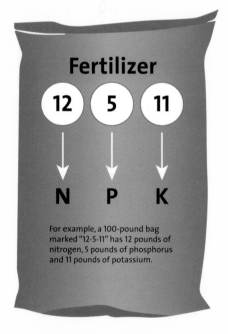

Fertilizer

12 5 11

N P K

For example, a 100-pound bag marked "12-5-11" has 12 pounds of nitrogen, 5 pounds of phosphorus and 11 pounds of potassium.

Use fertilizers with low numbers, all below 20.

Cutting off, or deadheading, spent flowers before they can form seeds is a simple way to frustrate the plant's objective and trigger a new flush of bloom.

removed before seed is set, and so the cycle goes until either the plant or the gardener gives up. This intervention in the natural process extends the blooming period without damaging the plant.

A little fertilizer may also help pump out some more flowers, but if you go this route, be sure not to provide anything with a high amount of nitrogen. Too much nitrogen can shut down flowering, increasing stem and leaf growth at the expense of blossom production. However, a fertilizer with a higher amount of phosphorus (the middle number) will encourage bud set, and that means more flowers.

Fertility

Perennial plants have a good attitude about food. They prefer a meal of high-quality organic foods in the soil rather than quick-fix snacks from a box or a bottle. Manufactured fertilizers have their uses, but strong plants rely first on finding the basic building blocks of nutrition in home ground. Plants absorb nutrients through their roots and send them up to the leaves where they are combined with ultraviolet light to manufacture carbohydrate energy. This thrifty and convenient system, called photosynthesis, requires only that the gardener maintain a healthy soil with an annual addition of organic materials and consistent moisture.

Fertile soil has two essential characteristics: It contains sufficient quantities of the basic mineral plant foods (nitrogen, phosphorus and potassium) and a moist, humusy and crumbly texture that makes the nutrients available to roots. Most average garden soils have sufficient quantities of the main nutrients, as well as the trace elements that are also necessary for growth. Nitrogen is the one nutrient most readily leached from the soil by water; fortunately, it isn't required in large amounts. But every garden's soil needs replenishment of organic materials that are consumed by microbes and plants and must be regularly replaced. Renewing the organic content of your soil frequently by digging leaves, compost, peat moss, grass clippings, pine needles and aged manure into planting holes and using an organic mulch of leaves or shredded bark on the soil surface is a good way to ensure your plants will have strong growth.

Low-maintenance Roses

'America' climbing rose
H/W 10 feet (3 m); 3 inches (8 cm)
−20°F (−29°C)
Double coral flowers, disease-resistant, medium fragrance. Sun.

'Carefree Beauty' shrub rose
H/W 4 feet (1.2 m); 4 inches
(10 cm) −30°F (−34°C)
Semi-double pink flowers, disease-resistant, very fragrant. Sun.

'John Davis' climbing rose
H 6 feet (1.8 m) W 3 feet (1 m);
3 inches (8 cm) −30°F (−34°C)
Clusters of double, frilly pink flowers, disease-resistant, few thorns, slightly fragrant. Sun.

Knock Out ('*Rosa* x 'Radrazz')
shrub rose
H/W 4 feet (1.2 m); 3 inches (8 cm)
−20°F (−29°C)
Deep-pink flowers in hot climates, red in cooler temperatures, slight fragrance. Sun.

'Morden Sunrise' shrub rose
H 4 feet (1.2 m) W 3 feet (1 m);
4 inches (10 cm) −40°F (−40°C)
Semi-double yellow-orange flowers, disease-resistant, medium fragrance. Sun.

'Westerland' climbing rose

H 10 feet (3 m) W 3 feet (1 m) −20°F
(−29°C); 5 inches (12 cm)
Semi-double orange-pink flowers, disease-resistant, strong fragrance. Sun.

Low Maintenance Perennials

There is an abundance of low-maintenance perennials that bloom for extended periods over the summer. Tall and bushy plants include the sun-loving 'Taplow Blue' globe thistle (*Echinops ritro* 'Taplow Blue'), which has tall stems and rounded heads of densely packed tubular florets, and the double perennial sunflower (*Helianthus* x *multiflorus* 'Plenus'), with double pom-pom heads of bright gold flowers; 'Gateway' Joe-pye weed (*Eupatorium* 'Gateway'), which likes sun to part shade and has rosy-pink flowers that attract butterflies; and 'Lavender Mist' meadow rue, (*Thalictrum rochebrunianum* 'Lavender Mist'), which has see-through wispy blue-green foliage and slender stalks of pink-mauve clustered flowers and likes moist soil and part shade to dappled shade.

Perennials of medium height include sun-loving yellow foxglove (*Digitalis grandiflora*), 'Crimson Star' purple coneflower (*Echinacea purpurea* 'Crimson Star') and 'Sunny Border Blue' veronica (*Veronica* 'Sunny Border Blue'), while both the balloon flower (*Platycodon grandifloras*), with star-shaped blue flowers, and Jacob's ladder (*Polemonium caeruleum*), with lavender-blue flowers, like sun to part shade.

Perennial sunflower

Taplow Blue (globe thistle)

Yellow foxglove

Crimson star (purple coneflower)

Watering New Landscape Plants

The growth of perennial plants is reliant on three simple factors: soil, light and moisture. It would seem that almost any garden could provide these basics. Although circumstances of poor soil quality and low light often conspire to skew the growth equation, plants do make an effort to increase their size in less than perfect conditions. But while plants can go a long way to overcome shortcomings in the garden, there is no compensation for inadequate moisture. Water is life to plants. Newly installed plants require watering three times a week during the first growing season, with enough water to wet the entire root ball all the way to the bottom. In periods of drought combined with high heat and wind, daily watering is necessary.

Stem elongation and bud development are initiated by root growth, and root growth is initiated by soil moisture. The growth of plant roots is informed by a genetic strategy—grow only toward sustenance. A perennial plant does not put roots out into dry soil and stays instead within its current root mass, shutting down any effort at aboveground expansion. In the absence of life-sustaining water, plants retreat to triage behavior by dropping flower buds and canceling summer plans.

> Newly installed plants require watering three times a week during the first growing season, with enough water to wet the entire root ball all the way to the bottom.

Check Your Soil Regularly

The answer to this scenario is to provide adequate and consistent moisture. Plants are not electric lights—their productivity can't be turned on and off without performance being seriously affected. The demands of our daily lives (working late at the office, dropping the kids off at a play date, taking the cat to the vet) can easily overtake the few moments necessary to stoop down and feel the soil. But losing touch with your soil's moisture content can quickly result in arrested plant growth. And the bad news is, plants are reluctant to switch back into growth mode if water availability is erratic. Check your soil regularly.

Water delivery is partly based on weather conditions. Less water is required in spring and autumn when cool temperatures help to maintain moisture in the soil. More water is used by plants and evaporates in the heat of summer. As well, soil texture has a strong influence on how frequently you need to provide water.

> Plants are reluctant to switch back into growth mode if water availability is erratic.

Planting for Two Bursts of Bloom in One Location

Slender deutzia

Showy stonecrop

Pairing shrubs and perennials that bloom at different times helps to economize on space and creates a visual change without adding to your work. Here are a few suggestions for how to apply this principle in your new garden.

The Slender Deutzia (*Deutzia gracilis*) grows to a height of 3 feet (1 m) and a spread of 4 feet (1.2 m), is hardy to –20°F (–29°C). In May, it has masses of frilly white flowers on its arching branches. Pair it with the very hardy autumn-blooming showy stonecrop (*Sedum spectabile*), which grows to 18 inches (45 cm) in sun to part shade and comes in colors such as dusty pink 'Autumn Joy,' rosy magenta 'Neon' or white 'Stardust.'

The Early-blooming 5-foot (1.5 m) Ottawa Early forsythia (*Forsythia ovata* 'Ottawa' has bright yellow flowers and is hardy to –30°F (–34°C). Pair it with 3-foot (90 cm) sun-loving, autumn-blooming 'Honorine Jobert' Japanese Anemone (*Anemone* x *hybrida*), which has white flowers with yellow centers, or with rose-pink 'September Charm.'

White bleedingheart

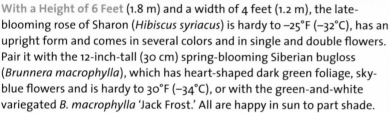

Bridalwreath spirea

With a Height of 6 Feet (1.8 m) and a width of 4 feet (1.2 m), the late-blooming rose of Sharon (*Hibiscus syriacus*) is hardy to –25°F (–32°C), has an upright form and comes in several colors and in single and double flowers. Pair it with the 12-inch-tall (30 cm) spring-blooming Siberian bugloss (*Brunnera macrophylla*), which has heart-shaped dark green foliage, sky-blue flowers and is hardy to 30°F (–34°C), or with the green-and-white variegated *B. macrophylla* 'Jack Frost.' All are happy in sun to part shade.

The 4-foot Tall (1.2 m) bridalwreath spirea (*Spiraea prunifolia*) has small blue-green foliage on arching branches, is smothered with bright white flowers in spring and is hardy to –30°F (–34°C). Pair it with 18-inch-tall (45 cm) fern-leaf bleeding heart (*Dicentra formosa* hybrids), which is hardy to –40°F (–40°C) and comes in several colors, such as ruby-red 'Adrian Bloom,' rose-red 'King of Hearts' and ivory-white 'Langtrees.' All are happy in sun to part shade.

Rose of Sharon

With its Open Shape, slender branches and brilliant true-pink flowers in early spring, the 'Olga Mezitt' rhododendron (*Rhododendron* hybrids) has a height and spread of 5 feet (1.5 m) and is hardy to –30°F (–34°C). 'Aglo' rhododendron has light pink flowers with red throats. Pair with autumn-blooming lavender-blue Michaelmas daisies (*Aster novae-angliae* 'Hella Lacy') or rose-pink 'Pink Winner,' which both grow to 36 inches (90 cm), enjoy part shade and are hardy to –40°F (–40°C).

With Creamy White Flowers, *Hydrangea paniculata* 'Unique' grows to a height of 5 feet (1.5 m) and a width of 6 feet (1.8 m) and is hardy to –20°F (–29°C). Also try dwarf *H. paniculata* 'Bombshell' with white flowers turning to pink. Pair the midsummer blooming hydrangea with spring-blooming columbine (*Aquilegia* hybrid 'McKana's Giant'), which grows to 36 inches (90 cm), comes in many color combinations and is hardy to –40°F (–40°C). They like sun to part shade.

Siberian bugloss

A soaker hose is the most efficient way of getting water to plants with minor labor for the gardener.

Keeping the water delivery low down and in the largest droplet size possible maximizes the amount that penetrates the soil.

Sandy soil drains rapidly, and irrigation is required more frequently. Heavier soil with more clay content is slower to release water and can bank it in the root zone for longer periods. Consistency in your irrigation schedule can only be developed if you monitor the soil moisture in your garden and get a feel for how rapidly or slowly it is depleted.

How much moisture should you provide? There's no point in tantalizing plants with just enough water to darken the soil surface. Many perennial plants have roots that reach a depth of 10 inches (25 cm), and you should aim for "sponge-damp" moisture at that level. Dig a hole and feel for moisture in the root zone. It shouldn't be soupy at any level. But soil at the bottom of an 8-to-10-inch (20–25 cm) hole should have the moisture of a wrung-out sponge.

And how should moisture be delivered? Water flung about in the air by various whirly devices or oscillating bars powering 8-foot (2.5 m) waves of droplets can be counted on for a great show, but these devices lose a major amount of water to evaporation. The basic rule is the higher a droplet of water travels through the air, the greater the amount of evaporation and a corresponding decline in the amount that will reach the root zone. Keeping the water delivery low down and in the largest droplet size possible maximizes the amount that penetrates the soil. Watering with a slow hose at ground level is a good way to deliver water to perennials and explore their new developments in the process.

But if you haven't time to spend with the plants, the next best thing to being there is a soaker hose laid through the bed. Soaker hoses efficiently "sweat" water out in slow large droplets and can run for several hours. They conserve water, avoid wastage and deliver moisture where it belongs—in the root zone. Put one down and turn it on, then watch for the darkened areas of soil that show you where the water is going. Adjust the placement of the hose to reach your target plants, and then slip away for some planter's punch. No one would blame you.

Organic Mulch

Finally, the single most important improvement you can make in the garden is organic mulch around your perennial plants. A 2-inch (5 cm) layer of shredded leaves, shredded bark, pine needles or grass clippings will suppress weed growth, lower soil temperature in summer heat and preserve water in the root zone by inhibiting evaporation from the surface. This is definitely the smart way to garden, and you'll have the gratification of bounteous blooms as a reward.

If you have installed an underground irrigation system in the garden, you'll encounter the intricacies of setting the area zones and the duration of time they receive water. Begin relying on the irrigation system when spring is well established and days have developed warm afternoons. The first order of business is to make sure water is delivered in early-morning hours before the sun has risen in the sky. The sun heats the air as it climbs its arc, causing convection winds to blow and evaporate water droplets before they have a chance to sink into the soil. (There is nothing more useless than delivering droplets of water in bright sun on a windy day.) Set the control system to allow maximum watering time for each garden zone, because what seems like a thorough drenching may be quickly sucked up by day's end. Check to see how much water is penetrating into the root zone by digging a discrete 8-inch (20 cm) hole and feeling the soil at bottom. It should feel sponge-damp. If not, adjust the length of time water is delivered in that zone, or plan on irrigating more frequently.

Make sure water is delivered in early-morning hours before the sun has risen in the sky.

Weeding methods

There are two easy ways to break the weed cycle. One is to keep earth turning to a minimum—every turned shovel of soil exposes weed seeds to light and potential germination. The second is to shade the soil from sunlight. Covering all exposed soil and the roots of shrubs and trees with organic mulch, which prevents light

from reaching weed seeds underground, dramatically reduces the appearance of new weeds. Spread a thick 4-inch (10 cm) layer, topping it up with roughly 2 inches (5 cm) more each year.

Remove the weeds before putting down the mulch. Mulch can be put down at any time of year. Afterwards, the mulch only needs to be topped up annually, and the occasional aggressive weed that makes its way through removed.

If weeds are a chronic problem in your garden and you don't have time to work on their removal, follow this one important rule—never allow them to go to seed. If you notice a patch of weeds in flower, go out every day and pull off the flowers. That effectively eliminates a new crop of baby weeds and buys you some time until you can really work at their removal.

To get rid of weeds permanently, you must remove at least two-thirds of the root. Removing the leaves of mature weeds is wasted effort, as they can regrow fully in three weeks using energy stored in the roots. Removing weed seedlings that haven't yet developed thick taproots can be done with a small-bladed hoe, though there are variations specifically designed for weeding that can be purchased at a garden center or the hardware section at larger stores. With experience, you'll soon determine what is the most effective weeding tool for your purpose.

Of course, the day dawns when you must get down on the ground and begin weeding by hand. Protect your knees with strap-on knee pads or some kind of kneeling pad. The secret to removing mature weeds easily and with the crucial two-thirds of the root attached is this: make sure the soil is wet. Save your weeding time for immediately after a heavy rain, or use a garden hose to saturate your designated work area. The taproots of weeds grow fine filaments along their length, which anchor the plant in the ground. A thorough soaking of the soil releases their grip, and the plant will slide out as if greased. Slide your tool of choice down vertically alongside the weed's root, nudge it slightly to loosen the root, then grasp the crown of the plant (not the foliage), and slowly pull upward. You'll be able to feel what's going on underground; if there's too much resistance, give the root another nudge and try again. After 30 minutes' work, you'll have a rewarding pile of limp weeds at your side.

To get rid of weeds permanently you must get rid of at least two-thirds of the root.

Save your weeding time for immediately after a heavy rain, or use a garden hose to saturate your designated work area.

Covering all exposed soil and the roots of shrubs and trees with organic mulch, which prevents light from reaching weed seeds underground, dramatically reduces the appearance of new weeds.

Best Carpeting Ground-Cover Plants

Ground-cover plants are a big category and include plants up to 3 feet (1 m) high. The most efficient at weed suppression are the low-growing carpet ground covers, plants with expanding cushions of dense leaves or stems that creep outward and root from their leaf axels as they travel along. The resulting network of foliage forms a carpet that shades the soil and prevents weed seeds from germinating. Combined with a few artistically placed small boulders, carpets of ground cover make an attractive display, adding texture and ornamental detail to empty garden space.

1 Sweet woodruff (*Galium odoratum*)

H 8 inches (20 cm) −40°F (−40°C)
Carpeting mats of finely formed star-shaped foliage with bright, sweetly fragrant white flowers in spring. Requires moist, organic soil. Will not grow in bright sun and remains green deep into winter. Sun to part shade.

2 Creeping lily turf (*Liriope spicata*)

H 10 inches (25 cm) −20°F (−29°C)
Narrow grass-like leaves forming thick mats with pale lilac flower spikes. Lily turf is a vigorous plant spreading by underground rhizomes and can be invasive. Good under trees where nothing else will grow. The beautiful cultivar 'Silver Dragon' has silver-white banding. Sun to part shade in well-drained soil.

3 Wintergreen (*Gaultheria procumbens*)

H 4 inches (10 cm) −20°F (−29°C)
Creeping stems of glossy evergreen leaves with pinkish white flowers and lovely red fruits. Winter foliage color is mahogany-red, and the entire plant is pleasantly scented with wintergreen fragrance. Part shade and acidic soil (pH 4.5 to 5.5).

4 Lily-of-the-valley (*Convallaria majalis*)

H 8 inches (20 cm) −40°F (−40°C).
Broad green leaf blades grow tightly packed to cover ground; needs consistently moist soil to remain green through summer. Stems of deeply perfumed white bell flowers in spring; good for woodland gardens and narrow shady path borders. Tends to be invasive. Shade.

5 Moneywort, or creeping Jenny (*Lysimachia nummularia*)

H 3 inches (8 cm) −30°F (−34°C)
A creeping plant with long strands of glossy leaves that root at the joints and bright yellow flowers in summer. The cultivar 'Aurea' has yellow foliage, is less vigorous and prefers shade. Sun to part shade in moist soil.

6 Lamb's ears (*Stachys byzantina*)

H 6 inches (15 cm) −20°F (−29°C)
A mat-forming plant with gray-green wooly leaves and purple flower spikes in summer. The cultivar 'Silver Carpet' is silver-gray and non-flowering; 'Helen von Stein' has the largest foliage. Another gray-leaved plant is snow-in-summer (*Cerastium tomentosum*), with brilliant white flowers in spring and small silver leaves that form dense carpets. Sun in dry soil.

Easy-Care Ground-Cover Plants

These low-maintenance ground-cover plants (all under 12 in/30 cm) are reliably self-reliant. Put them in the right conditions, and they will spread to cover soil and keep weeds out.

1 European wild ginger (*Asarum europaeum*)

H 6 inches (15 cm) W 24 inches (60 cm) −20°F (−29°C)
Glossy green leaves overlapping to form dense cushions on flat or sloped surfaces, attractive and no maintenance. Prefers moist soil. Sun to part shade.

2 Coral bells (*Heuchera sanguinea*)

H 10 inches (25 cm) W 18 inches (45 cm) −20°F (−29°C)
Clump-forming plants in green, bronze, plum and near-black, with thin stems of colorful summer-blooming bell flowers waving above. Grouped together, these charming plants spread out to form a wide skirt of leaves. Look for 'Amber Waves' (amber-gold), 'Green Spice' (green and white) and 'Purple Sails' (plum). Sun to part shade.

3 Snow-in-summer (*Cerastium tomentosum*)

H 6 inches (15 cm) W 18 inches (45 cm) −40°F (−40°C)
Dense cushions of fuzzy olive-green to gray-white leaves, soft texture, with white flower spikes in spring. Needs good drainage and will grow in hot, dry soil. Sun.

4 Foamflower (*Tiarella cordifolia*)

H 6 inches (15 cm) W 18 inches (45 cm) −35°F (−37°C)
Foamflower spreads in moist soil by underground runners to form clumps of low leaves with airy sprays of white or pale pink flowers. *Tiarella* is a native woodland plant that has been hybridized. Look for 'Running Tapestry' (green leaves with red veins and pink flowers). Several fancy and non-spreading cultivars also available. Part shade.

5 Barrenwort (*Epimedium* spp)

H 12 inches (30 cm) W 18 inches (45 cm) −20°F (−29°C)
Dense clump-forming plants with overlapping leaves and wiry stems of flowers in spring. The variety 'Rubrum' has red-tinged leaves and bright carmine flowers; *E.* x *youngianum* 'Niveum' has white flowers. Barrenwort is a dependable ground cover in dry shade and attractive all summer. Shade.

6 Spotted deadnettle (*Lamium maculatum*)

H 8 inches (20 cm) W 24 inches (60 cm) −40°F (−40°C)
Rambling stems with mat-forming, small green foliage edged white or pewter-gray. Flowers are pink, white or rosy-purple in spring through early summer. Sun to part shade.

Growing Annuals & Perennials

SHOP FOR ANNUAL PLANTS EARLY IN THE SPRING PLANTING season, when the transplants are fresh and in optimum condition. Greenhouse growers deliver healthy plants to garden centers, and it's smart to get them early, before they deteriorate waiting for sale. Most summer-blooming annuals are sold as small transplants in cell packs.

Always buy healthy cell packs of starter plants. The foliage should be clean and facing upward toward light. Avoid plants that have spotted and diseased leaves. Purchasing diseased plants simply imports those problems into your garden.

Avoid plants that have been waiting too long in their cell packs and grown tall and leggy. Their root systems will be thickly congested and may cause the plant's growth to be permanently stunted.

The transplants should be standing firmly upright, with no signs of wilt. The cell pack of plants should not feel almost weightless with dry soil but have the weight of recent watering.

When planting annuals into a garden bed, first cultivate the soil to give them a soft place to set out new roots. If the root systems have been constrained and gathered on the sides of the root balls, gently break apart the section of massed roots in one or two places, so that new roots can find a way out. Set the plants into the soil at the same depth they've been growing in their cell packs,

Always buy healthy cell packs of starter plants. The foliage should be clean and facing upward toward light. Avoid plants that have spotted and diseased leaves.

with the neck of each plant at soil level. Gently firm them in with your hands, and water well with a gentle spray that won't knock them over. Using a liquid transplant fertilizer will get them off to a quick start.

Groom plants weekly, removing any damaged or diseased foliage and all spent or finished flowers. Allowing finished flowers to remain on plants triggers seed production and slows the development of flower buds. Deadheading is the best way to keep plants flowering.

Pinching out the growing tips from annuals helps tall, leggy plants develop a bushier form with increased flowering potential. If new transplants are excessively leggy, pinch just a half-inch (1.3 cm) from the growing tips to encourage side shoots and better form. Plants like petunias that have been growing and blooming for several weeks into midsummer and have grown lanky will benefit if you pinch their stems back by one-third to one-half, which causes side branches to grow with new flower production. Whenever you pinch plants, provide a fertilizer feeding to help speed regenerative growth of new stems and flower buds.

Congested root systems may cause a plant's growth to be stunted permanently. Look for packs with light rooting, as on the left.

Deadheading is important to keep annuals flowering all season long. Remove spent flowers and seed heads.

To stimulate more side branching and make a bushier plant, clip or pinch out the growing tips. This will stimulate hidden buds along the branch or stem, resulting in fresh growth and a fuller form.

Keep the plants flowering heavily by providing water-soluble fertilizer every third week.

Annual summer-blooming plants are intended to provide a large and consistent number of flowers in a spring-to-autumn growing season. Keep the plants flowering heavily by providing water-soluble fertilizer every third week. To promote root growth and increase flower bud production, use a fertilizer product with a higher middle number (such as 5-15-5). A balanced fertilizer (such as 10-10-10) is also acceptable. Fertilizers with a higher first number (such as 19-6-12) promote leaves at the expense of flower buds and are appropriate for foliage plants like coleus.

Plants in Containers

Every plant container must have at least one drainage hole in the bottom to allow excess water to escape. If you want to use a decorative container, first put the plant into a drained pot that will fit into the larger container. Plants in pots without drainage are deprived of the oxygen they take from the soil, and that is rapidly fatal.

For temporary seasonal plants in pots, use a lightweight soilless mix sold in bags purchased at a garden center. This peat-based mix is sterile and carries no disease organisms or insect larvae.

Containers that are standing in direct sunlight hold heat in the soil mix, which causes environmental stress to plant roots. (The soil surrounding plant roots in the ground is significantly cooler than in containers.) If plants in consistent sun are wilting or showing scorched spots on foliage despite regular watering, move the containers to a partial-sun location with no more than three or four hours of direct sunlight.

Containers in full sun or windy locations may require daily watering at the height of summer. To conserve the water in the container soil, mulch each pot with a 1-to-2-inch (2.5–5 cm) layer of shredded bark on the soil surface. Plastic pots hold soil moisture longer. Terracotta clay pots transpire water rapidly through the walls but can be lined with plastic to prevent moisture evaporation. Cut the bottom seam from a plastic bag that will comfortably fit into a clay pot, creating an open top and bottom. Press the bag against the walls of the pot and fill with planting mix. Settle the plants into the pot, and cut off the excess length of plastic an inch (2.5 cm) above soil level. The extra inch of plastic film at top will guide water into the soil and prevent loss of moisture down the sides. As plants grow, they will conceal the edge of plastic around the pot wall.

Fill containers with fresh soilless mix in spring. Old soil mix should be emptied and spread across garden beds at the end of the season. If you save soil mix, you'll also save fungus spores and insect larvae that can infest new plants next season.

Plants in pots without drainage are deprived of the oxygen they take from the soil, and that is rapidly fatal.

Perennial Beds

Perennial beds can be as easy or as complicated as you choose to make them. Start out with a collection of easy-to-grow, reliably cold-hardy plants that will return each year. Select plants that grow bigger by enlarging their clump size, and avoid those with running roots that expand and colonize new areas.

The textbook method is to plant the tallest and bushiest perennials (such as perennial sunflower and globe thistle) at the back of the bed, and work forward with descending plant heights. But there are often opportunities to do things differently, and if you're planting tall, slender plants (such as delphiniums and hollyhocks), it's possible to move them closer to the front without blocking the view of things growing behind.

Keep in mind that perennial plants enjoy company in relaxed groupings based on triangular formations. Setting plants of the same kind in a three-point formation with space to grow between

Fill containers with fresh soilless mix in spring. Old soil mix should be emptied and spread across garden beds at the end of the season.

Best Spring-Flowering Bulbs, Corms and Tubers

In the earliest spring days, we still have a long wait before the first leaves sprout from the bare branches of lonely woody shrubs and trees. Spring-flowering bulbs and woodland plants can be naturalized to provide a reliable show of fresh foliage and blossoms as early as late winter. Not all bulbs, corms and tubers are reliably perennial, though some will appear indefinitely through the years, and their numbers increase over time.

These plants all naturalize easily and can be left to roam through beds and borders and even into the lawn. They naturalize more rapidly if planted in generous clusters, the bulbs almost touching each other. In moist soil, new colonies of self-sown seedlings should appear within four or five years, then spread more rapidly. Always leave foliage to ripen to at least half-brown before removing, which ensures that enough energy is stored in the bulb for reproduction. Let stems with seed heads remain until dry and their contents have spilled into the garden. If small bulbs, such as scilla and species crocus, are planted in the lawn, resist mowing until their foliage has fully ripened. Letting the grass grow tall and shaggy in spring promotes deep root growth and drought-hardiness.

1 Tulip (*Tulipa* spp & hybrids)

H 6 to 30 inches (15–75 cm)
These smaller, early-blooming species tulips return over many years if their foliage is allowed to ripen, although they won't spread like the minor bulbs. The intense yellow-and-white *T. tarda* opens and closes with the sun and *T. saxatilis* 'Lilac Wonder' is lilac-pink with yellow and white. Try also *T. pulchella* 'Violacea,' *T. sylvestris* and *T. acuminata*. The larger Darwin hybrids return for a decade.

2 Glory-of-the-snow (*Chionodoxa* spp)

H 3 to 8 inches (7–20 cm)
This blue-and-white spring beauty lifts spirits in the last days of winter. Plant it under trees, where it looks particularly lovely with dark blue scilla (*Scilla siberica*) and blue-striped white Siberian squills (*Puschkinia*).

3 Crocus (*Crocus* spp & hybrids)

H 1 to 10 inches (2.5–25 cm)
The earliest small crocus, sometimes referred to as snow crocus, blooms for many years in the garden. This colorful group contains species and simple hybrids of wild bulbs. Look for two-toned *C. tommasinianus* 'Barr's Purple,' yellow, white and purple *C. sieberi* 'Tricolor,' and *C. chrysanthus* 'Gypsy Girl' (yellow and maroon), 'Prins Claus' (royal purple) and 'Lady Killer' in white and purple. Blooms at the same time as blue scilla (*Scilla siberica*).

4 Snowdrop (*Galanthus* spp & hybrids)

H 3 to 9 inches (7–23 cm)
Snowdrops are up in late winter or earliest spring and appear when the ground is still frozen. Their nodding opaque white flowers are especially brilliant clustered as a skirt around the dark branches of evergreens such as yew and boxwood. Reliable *G. nivalis* prefers moist soil in light shade to part sun, spreading slowly. Showier giant *G. elwesii* and double *G. nivalis* 'Flore Pleno' do not spread.

5 Virginia bluebells (*Mertensia virginica*)

H 18 inches (45 cm)
The lobed blue-green foliage of bluebells rises early in spring, followed by clusters of bright blue bells. They live for many years in shade or sun and need moist soil to spread. Fellow bloomers are trumpet daffodils, and the species Narcissus will increase and naturalize in meadowlike conditions in full sun and in soil that is moist in spring, drier in summer.

6 Grape hyacinth (*Muscari* spp & hybrids)

H 4 to 8 inches (10–20 cm)
Cold-hardy and easy-growing, deep blue Muscari are lovely with yellow Narcissus and trout lilies. In time, the grapelike blue clusters of *M. neglectum* and *M. azureum* form drifts through a garden bed or shrub border. Cultivars include white *M. botryoides* 'Album,' two-toned blue *M. tubergianum* 'Oxford and Cambridge' and the strangely fluffy *M. armeniacum* 'Fantasy Creation.'

Best Summer Annuals

At the garden center, you'll find such a large selection of plants—from old-fashioned favorites your grandmother grew to the latest hybrids—that you'll have a hard time making a selection.

Annuals are genetically programmed to excel in flower production over a 20-week season, and almost any annual plant produces an avalanche of flowers as long as it has found its place in the sun (or shade). The trick lies in finding the place that gets them the optimal amount of light—or close enough.

Because of their high flower production, annual plants also demand sufficient water. Petal tissues require more water than leaf tissues to remain turgid and in good condition.

Along with their requirement for regular and generous amounts of water, annuals appreciate feeding with commercially prepared water-soluble fertilizer solutions to support their high energy requirements. Feeding with a 10-15-10 fertilizer every second week will keep them bursting with bloom all season.

1 Zinnia (*Zinnia angustifolia*, *Z. elegans* and *Z. haageana*)

H 12 to 48 inches (30–120 cm)
A variety of single-, double- and cactus-flowered plants with many branching side stems and blossoms in every color except blue. As with all annuals, remove the spent flowers to keep buds coming. Zinnias are heat-loving plants that are ideal for locations in bright sun.

2 Coleus (*Solenostemon scutellarioides* syn *Coleus blumei*)

Flower spikes H 10 to 24 inches (25–60 cm)
The coleus is available in a wide range of colorful and intriguingly patterned foliage in many shades of red, purple, pink, yellow and black, with varieties being developed regularly. Pinch early in the summer to encourage branching. If you want ornamental display beyond the valuable foliage, allow the flower spikes to develop. Part sun to light shade.

3 Busy Lizzie, patience plant (*Impatiens walleriana*)

H 12 to 24 inches (30–60 cm)
Mounding plants with brilliantly colored single or double flowers that bloom from late spring until the first frost. Impatiens plants require humus-rich soil and consistent moisture. They should not be allowed to dry out in hot weather. Part sun to light shade.

4 Begonia (*Begonia*)

H 8 to 24 inches (20–60 cm)
The larger begonias grow from tubers, while the smaller bedding begonias have fibrous roots. These bright flowers bloom all summer and into autumn in consistently moist (but not wet) soil. Be sure to provide water in hot spells. They bring vivid color to part sun and light shade conditions.

5 Spider flower (*Cleome hassleriana*)

H 60 inches (150 cm)
These distinctive plants have airy, ball-shaped flowers in purple, rose, pink or white atop long, arching 48-inch (120 cm) stems. They are useful at the back of a border or between tall shrubs. Spider flowers will tolerate dry soil, and they self-seed easily. Full sun to part shade.

6 Scarlet sage (*Salvia splendens*)

H 12 to 36 inches (30–90 cm)
Sturdy upright plants with central and side flower spikes in shades of purple, red and white, with other colors increasingly available. Deadhead spent blooms frequently and promptly so that plants keep producing flower spikes. This is a true heat-loving plant that requires full sun. However, the cultivars in pastel colors, such as 'Sizzler Series,' require some shelter from full sun.

Plant the tallest and bushiest perennials, such as this globe thistle, at the back of the bed. Although tall, slender plants such as delphiniums and hollyhocks can be planted closer to the front.

them allows plants to fill in and mass together, making a pleasantly generous clump of foliage and flowers within an informal setting. In a space that allows for more than one plant, try to get plants in odd-numbered groups—three, five, seven and so on— and set them in triangular arrangements with shared sides.

Basic Perennial Maintenance

Looking after plants has more to do with pleasure than with work, although traditional terms such as "yard work" and "landscape maintenance" don't do much to encourage the spirit of gardening. Make it easier on yourself by judiciously setting a few flat stones in the bed that you can use as a stable surface when deadheading, removing damaged foliage and pulling weeds. If you're interested in plants and want to know more about their characteristics and behavior, any form of maintenance is an opportunity to explore what they have to offer, and a close-up perspective from within the bed tells you a lot. At its best moments, plant maintenance is a rich encounter appealing to our senses of touch, scent and vision. So prepare yourself for a pleasant experience, don't rush to finish, and allow enough time to do the job right. The plants will repay your efforts many times over.

Pruning Simplified

Pruning is a puzzle to most gardeners—and with good reason. Every plant has a genetic plan for its final mature shape and size, and pruning isn't on the agenda. When gardening shears or pruners cut into living wood, buds lower down on the branch are activated to replace the lost wood. (With many woody plants, one cut will activate two dormant buds.) It's no wonder so many efforts to control plant size with pruning are frustrated by explosions of new growth.

Most shrubs and trees are bred in small, medium and large size. If you want to avoid pruning woody plants almost entirely, measure the available garden space and select plants that have a potential mature size that will fit the area.

Even so, pruning is a useful skill. Cutting at the correct time makes the difference between getting the results you want quickly and easily and engaging in a disappointing and time-consuming cycle of cut-and-cut-again. An overgrown shrub takes on a rangy, leggy shape; foliage appears more in some areas than in others; and blossoms, if any, also show inconsistently. Renovating a shrub kick-starts the plant, forcing its energy to be invested back into what it does best—producing foliage and blossoms and achieving its mature natural shape and size.

To keep the shrub at the same size: Allow the plant to spend its energy on spring growth, then cut back twigs and canes in early summer when little energy is left for replacement buds. Cut back no more than one-third of the plant's height and width.

To invigorate a sluggish plant and stimulate growth: In early spring before buds break, prune twigs lightly, removing no more than 10 percent of any branch or cane. This triggers replacement buds to help the shrub gain greater mass in spring.

Pruning can activate new bud growth.

Making the cut

Cutting wood on a 45-degree angle allows moisture to drain easily off the cut tip. Although you have cut only one twig or branch, two buds farther down the stem are then activated, replacing the cut wood at a 2-for-1 ratio. That's why pruning to reduce size often produces a plant of greater size than you started with. Selecting a plant with potential dimensions to fit the space available is less stressful (for both you and the plant) and more successful.

Best Perennials for April and May

A landscape is brought to life in early to mid-spring by the emerging leaves of fresh green perennials. Ideally, soft herbaceous plants partnered with woody shrubs at the foot of a hedge or within a foundation planting share certain characteristics: strong stems that don't require staking, a long period of bloom and a natural resistance to insects and diseases.

Be generous with the numbers of spring perennials in your garden. Drifts and sheets of color are what revive the gardener's spirit after a long winter, and many spring perennials have low-growing foliage that can continue to be attractive all summer, long after their blooms have faded. If the leaves of cranesbill geranium become tatty in midsummer, they can be cut back to stimulate a new flush of foliage that will last until frost. The foliage of columbines and pinks also continues to be ornamental until the snow flies.

1 Moss phlox (*Phlox subulata*)

H 6 inches (15 cm) −40°F (−40°C)
Creeping mat-forming plants with star-shaped single flowers in brilliant shades of pink, cerise, blur or white, many with contrasting eye. Good ground cover in a rock garden and will cascade over the edge of a retaining wall. Sun to part shade.

2 Jacob's ladder (*Polemonium caeruleum*)

H 30 inches (75 cm) −30°F (−34°C)
Attractive ladder-like foliage and tall stems of long-lasting blue flowers. 'Snow and Sapphires' has green leaves lined in cream and rich violet-blue flowers. Creeping *Polemonium reptans* 'Blue Pearl' grows to 10 inches (25 cm) and is a good ground cover.

3 Primrose (*Primula vulgaris*)

H 8 inches (20 cm) −20°F (−29°C)
Simple open-faced primroses and cowslips (*P. veris*) are lovely with perennial hellebores (*Hellebore niger* and *H. orientalis*) and small early bulbs like blue scilla (*Scilla*) and blue-and-white glory-of-the-snow (*Chionodoxa*). Light shade to part sun.

4 Common bleedingheart (*Dicentra spectabilis*)

H 36 inches (90 cm) −30°F (−34°C)
Long wands of heart-shaped pink and white flowers spring about in breezes and continue blooming for four to six weeks. The all-white form is especially elegant. Prefers consistently moist soil with generous organic matter.

5 Bethlehem sage (*Pulmonaria saccharata*)

H 12 inches (30 cm) −30°F (−34°C)
Spreading stems with white spotted leaves and bell-like pink, blue and white flowers. There are many cultivars available, particularly pink 'Mrs. Moon' and white 'Spilled Milk,' with almost entirely white leaves. A very early riser in spring.

6 Columbine (*Aquilegia* spp)

H 10 to 36 inches (25-90 cm) −40°F (−40°C)
A delicate woodland gem with spurred flowers on stiff stems and blue-green foliage in late spring to early summer. Available with single or double flowers; some are bicolored. Needs moist organic soil in sun to part shade.

Best Perennials for June and July

With more than half of all perennials in bloom, June and July is a colorful time in the garden, which makes resilient, long-blooming perennials important assets. By removing spent flowers just as they finish blooming, it's possible to lengthen the blooming period for perennials by an average of two weeks. If browning flower heads are left on the plants, however, they soon begin producing seed and shut down flower production. Prompt deadheading frustrates their efforts to manufacture seed, resulting in more flushes of flower buds. Once your perennial plants are mature, they can be divided in late summer, when flowering is over.

All perennials benefit from regular watering but can withstand slightly dry locations. Expect longer blooming periods when plants have consistently moist soil enriched with leaves, peat moss and compost.

1 Shasta daisy (*Leucanthemum* x *superbum*)

H 12 to 24 inches (30–60 cm)
–20°F (–29°C)
There are many species and hybrids available of this classic white daisy with a yellow center disk, and the most familiar is 'Alaska,' with single 2-inch (5 cm) daisies on 24-inch (60 cm) stems. 'Aglaya' has frilly double flowers, and 'Little Miss Muffet' has semi-double blossoms on shorter stems (14 in/35 cm). 'Majestic' has the largest flowers (6 in/15 cm). Full sun.

2 Daylilies (*Hemerocallis* x *hybrida*)

H 10 to 40 inches (25–100 cm)
–40°F (–40°C)
An enormous range of daylilies is available in scarlet, apricot, yellow, peach and violet shades, many with scented or patterned petals and crimped "pie-crust" edges. 'Hyperion' is a pale yellow perfumed blossom that should be in every collection. Flowers are broad or narrow, some re-bloom, and the leaves make dense sword-shaped clumps. Full sun to part shade.

3 Cranesbill geranium (*Geranium* spp)

H 6 to 48 inches (15–120 cm)
–40°F (–40°C)
Not the traditional patio plant, the many cranesbill species are effective ground covers that flourish in situations from dry shade to full sun as clumps of attractive foliage, with flowers in white and many shades of pink, violet, blue and purple. 'Rozanne' is the longest blooming, with spreading wands of blue flowers all summer. Part shade to full sun.

4 Spike speedwell (*Veronica spicata*)

H 12 to 20 inches (30–50 cm)
–40°F (–40°C)
Bushy clumps with tall spikes of brilliantly colored flowers. 'Sunny Border Blue' has deep violet-blue branching spikes, while 'Red Fox' (or 'Rotfuchs') is bright rose-pink. Bright blue 'Royal Candles' H 8 to 12 inches (20–30 cm) is good for edging. Full sun.

5 Blanket flower (*Gaillardia* x *grandiflora*)

H 24 to 36 inches (60–90 cm)
–40°F (–40°C)
Cheerful, deep orange-and-yellow or maroon-russet daisylike flowers on a very vigorous plant that tolerates just about everything: drought, heat, cold, wind and poor soil. The rich colors of blanket flowers are useful to add a distinctive dark note to a perennial border, against which to accent other flowers in whites, blues, purples or pale yellow. Full sun.

6 Yarrow (*Achillea* spp)

H 18 to 48 inches (45–120 cm)
–40°F (–40°C)
These tall, sun-loving plants have flat clusters of tiny flowers in pink, yellow, rust, red and white. Deadhead spent flowers regularly for a long season of bloom. They are excellent for cut flowers, and the seed heads are ornamental in winter. Yarrow tolerates heavy soil and full sun.

Best Perennials for August and September

The last weeks of summer and the first weeks of early autumn typically bring cooler temperatures and moisture, renewing the partnership between woody plants and herbaceous perennials and extending the flowering season. Obedient plants and black-eyed Susans are still bright in the first weeks of September, and Michaelmas daisies and showy stonecrop are strong right up to the first hard frost.

When the leaves of perennials begin to turn brown, however, it's a signal that they are no longer producing energy for the plant. Depending on your taste, you can cut them back to the ground, leaving just a 2-inch (5 cm) stubble. Oversized clumps can either be divided now or left to be split in early spring. Alternatively, you can let clumps of the latest-blooming plants stand through winter, where they serve as attractive features in the snow.

1 Rose-mallow (*Hibiscus moscheutos*)

H 36 to 48 inches (90–120 cm)
–10°F (–23°C)
The "cold-climate hibiscus" has huge flowers (12 in/30 cm) on a shrub, blooming all summer to frost. 'Southern Belle' and 'Dixie Bell' are mixtures of red-, pink-, rose- and white-blooming plants. 'Lord Baltimore' is clear scarlet. Cut back hard in late fall, feed regularly, and provide it with shelter from the wind. Full sun to part shade.

2 Purple coneflower (*Echinacea purpurea*)

H 24 to 48 inches (60–120 cm)
–40°F (–40°C)
A bright plant with tall stems bearing pink-purple daisylike blooms with dark centers all summer long. Many cultivars are available in a range of colors (pink, purple, red, orange and white) in either single or double flowers. Leave the last flush of flowers to form seed heads, which are both ornamental in winter and very attractive to birds. Full sun to part shade.

3 Summer phlox (*Phlox paniculata*)

H 24 to 48 inches (60–120 cm)
–40°F (–40°C)
These mildew-resistant hybrids have small fragrant flowers in clear colors of pink, red, lavender, cerise and white. Full sun.

4 Michaelmas daisy (*Aster novi-belgii*)

H 12 to 36 inches (30–90 cm)
–30°F (–34°C)
The daisylike flowers of the Michaelmas come in pink, violet, blue or purple and sit on strong, branching stems. The mounding dwarf varieties are especially good for rock gardens. This daisy prefers cool, moist conditions in full sun.

5 Showy stonecrop (*Sedum spectabile*)

H 18 to 24 inches (45–60 cm)
–30°F (–34°C)
Succulent branching stems with gray-green leaves and long-lasting late-summer blooms that butterflies love. A good rock garden plant, stonecrop is drought-resistant and does well in full sun and part shade.

6 Black-eyed Susan (*Rudbeckia* spp)

H 24 to 60 inches (60–150 cm)
–30°F (–34°C)
Another well-loved daisylike flower that lights up a garden. Sunshine-yellow blooms with dark centers are excellent for cutting. Provide moist, loamy soil in part shade to full sun.

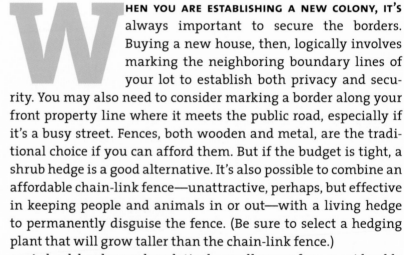

6 Trees & Shrubs

WHEN YOU ARE ESTABLISHING A NEW COLONY, IT'S always important to secure the borders. Buying a new house, then, logically involves marking the neighboring boundary lines of your lot to establish both privacy and security. You may also need to consider marking a border along your front property line where it meets the public road, especially if it's a busy street. Fences, both wooden and metal, are the traditional choice if you can afford them. But if the budget is tight, a shrub hedge is a good alternative. It's also possible to combine an affordable chain-link fence—unattractive, perhaps, but effective in keeping people and animals in or out—with a living hedge to permanently disguise the fence. (Be sure to select a hedging plant that will grow taller than the chain-link fence.)

A shrub border can be relatively small or run for a considerable length. Whatever the size of the bed you create, what matters is getting an interesting mix of plants with reasonable scale and dimensions that will have something ornamental to offer in all four seasons. Planning today for shrubs that are sizes your space can accommodate will eliminate many frustrating pruning jobs in the future. For instance, many of the famously beautiful French hybrid lilacs grow to 15 or 20 feet (4.5–6 m) in height, putting most of their flowers in the upper range. A shorter, partially

Fences, both wooden and metal, are the traditional choice if you can afford them. But if the budget is tight, a shrub hedge is a good alternative. Here we have both.

dwarf lilac topping out between 5 and 10 feet (1.5–3 m) has flowers much closer to your nose. Consider sun-loving Tinkerbelle dwarf lilac (*Syringa* 'Bailbelle'), with its spicy fragrance and wine-red buds; Sugar Plum Fairy (*S.* 'Bailsugar'), with lilac–pink flowers, and Fairy Dust (*S.* 'Baildust'), with pale pink flowers. Another dwarf lilac is 'Miss Kim' (*S. patula*), whose late-blooming flowers open in a shade of pale lavender-blue.

Choose evergreen and deciduous plants with colorful foliage—these are beautiful in the growing season and continue to keep the border attractive in snowy months. Also plan to include spring- and summer-flowering shrubs and plants with vibrant autumn colors. If space allows, you can also have plants with colorful bark and fruits for winter interest. A short border may only accommodate a few evergreen and deciduous flowering shrubs, while a longer border has space for repetition of some of the key plants.

For instance, in a long border, you could use three specimens of the same tall pyramidal evergreen—one at each end and another in the middle—to establish a cohesive pattern for winter. Taller coniferous shrubs for the border might include the

Prune spring flowering shrubs immediately after the blossoms are finished, and before they form next year's flower buds. If you wait more than three weeks after the flowers are finished, you'll lose next year's bloom.

What matters is getting an interesting mix of plants with reasonable scale and dimensions that will have something ornamental to offer in all four seasons.

Variegated dogwood

Hydrangeas

sun-loving, wind-resistant, pyramidal junipers *Juniperus chinensis* 'Fairview,' with bright green foliage, and 'Wichita Blue' juniper (*J. scopulorum*), with bright blue foliage. You should also consider 'Emerald' cedar (*Thuja occidentalis*), 'Europe Gold' cedar (*T. occidentalis*) and 'Rheingold' cedar (*T. occidentalis*), which respectively offer bright green foliage, golden yellow foliage and golden and bronze foliage.

Additional evergreens could be included, but that one key plant would be repeated to provide a design pattern for the border. A longer border also has space for shrubs with flowers blooming in spring and early and late summer, as well as plants with bright autumn color. Black chokeberry (*Aronia melanocarpa*) thrives in sun to part shade in wet or dry sandy soil. Its small green leaves turn brilliant scarlet in fall, and it has purple-black berries that attract birds. Ivory Halo dogwood (*Cornus alba* 'Bailho') has delicately textured green leaves edged in cream, blue-white berries and dark red winter twigs. Another dogwood, *C. sibirica* 'Sibirica Pearls,' has showy pure white berries and bright crimson branches in winter. The compact Show Off forsythia (*Forsythia* x *intermedia* 'Mindor') is covered with large brilliant yellow flowers in spring, while the Fire and Ice hydrangea (*Hydrangea paniculata* 'Wim's Red') has flower clusters that open in a creamy white, turning to raspberry pink in summer and deep red in fall. The Coppertina ninebark (*Physocarpus opulifolius* 'Mindia') has small maple-like leaves flushed with copper in spring and turning rich red in summer.

Put the taller plants toward the back and the shorter plants in front, and use both tall and short evergreens to establish a permanent bone structure that is visible in winter. Use the flowering shrubs between and in front of evergreens, and if you're including a few summer-flowering perennials or foliage plants like hostas, put them in the front row of the bed. You might also want to install some decorative rocks or small boulders, and those should be near the forward edge of the bed where they won't be covered by plant growth.

Your choice in shrubs for the lot lines is large. Starting with the most expensive, it includes evergreen conifers (like yew and cedar) that remain green year-round; flowering shrubs (like weigela, forsythia and garland spirea), which have a season of colorful bloom; and shrubs with green foliage but tiny or no flowers (like privet and dwarf burning bush) from spring through fall. It's also possible to use low-branching ornamental trees that have been bred to have narrow pyramidal forms with vertical branches which grow almost straight up (like hybrid ornamental pear and cherry trees), as well as attractive flower and fruit features.

Trees in Beds and Lawns

With the foundation bed and the lot lines secured with plant material, now you can relax and consider the issue of a tree for the front lawn or to anchor a large bed. Small dwarf trees with ornamental features, like a Lancelot crab apple (*Malus* 'Lanzam,' 10 feet/3 m) or Twisty Baby dwarf locust (*Robinia pseudoacacia* 'Lace Lady,' 8 feet/2.5 m), are appropriate vertical accents in garden beds and at the corner of a house in a foundation border, helping to tie a bed to the landscape and give it presence in four seasons. Dwarf trees have smaller root balls and won't force perennials and shrubs to compete for moisture.

A full-sized tree is a plant with strength, size and character, and its presence in a lawn area helps to balance the massive structure of your new home in the landscape. Placement of a lawn tree is entirely discretionary, and there is no reason for it to be set exactly in the middle of the lawn. In fact, it may easily be located closer to a prominent corner without actually interrupting the expanse of grass.

A lawn tree is not a shade tree in the old-fashioned sense of a large tree with dense foliage and deeply shaded areas under spreading branches. Trees with such size and structure, like the Norway maple (*Acer platanoides*) and its cultivars, have aggressive root systems, are highly competitive for light, moisture and nutrients and will degrade a grass lawn. An acceptable lawn tree has a compact form and a non-invasive root system, at most casting only dappled shade for a few hours. If you require a permanently shaded seating area, it's best to plan on constructing a simple pergola with room for shady vines over a brick patio or a canvas awning attached to a house wall. If an expansive shade tree holds a high position on your garden wish list, put it in the

Forsythia

Put the taller plants toward the back and the shorter plants in front.

backyard, and be prepared to accept its deleterious effect on other plantings.

A lawn tree is going to be one of a kind, and therefore it should have some special features, such as a season of flowering, as with a magnolia or crabapple; colorful foliage, as with the maroon-red Japanese maple (*Acer palmatum* 'Bloodgood'); ornamental bark, such as an exfoliating birch; or a distinctive form, like an architectural ginkgo tree. The lawn tree can also be a colorful conifer; be sure to look for one of the semi-dwarf versions under 25 feet/7.5 m, like 'Bakeri' blue spruce (*Picea pungens*), which won't tower over the house. Whatever your choice, the lawn tree should give you something of substance to look at in four seasons and remind you there is a garden out there even in the dead of winter.

How to Plant a Shrub

Shrubs can be weighty and are best moved in a wheelbarrow or a garden cart.

Grasping the shrub around the trunk to lift and carry it can sometimes result in a torn root system. If you can't move a heavy shrub in something with wheels, consider laying it on a tarp or old blanket so that two people can carry it sling fashion between them. Getting to the hole safely is half the job.

Before planting a shrub, trim off any broken twigs and determine which side is the front of the shrub. The front has a fuller profile and growth of branches fanning outward; the back is flatter. If the plant has had strong light from all directions during its growth, you may have difficulty discovering the true front, but one side may have better branch structure.

The advice for digging a hole for a shrub is similar to the advice for a perennial plant: It should be twice as deep and three times as wide as the root ball. Retain half the soil, and amend it with organic materials and coarse sand to bring the volume back to the original amount. The remaining portion of soil from the hole can be spread elsewhere in the bed. Add 2 cups (500 mL) of bonemeal to promote root growth. While shrubs planted without added soil amendments can certainly live, their growth is usually frustratingly slow because of the diminished amounts of oxygen and nutrients.

Lay the shrub on its side and firmly hold the trunk where it

Before planting a shrub, trim off any broken twigs and determine which side is the front of the shrub.

meets the top of the root ball while gently pulling away the container. If nothing budges, press gently on all sides of the container to loosen the root ball, and try again. If the plant has been in the container for too long, it may not be easily removed. In that case, use a heavy pair of garden clippers to cut off the container. Even if the container is made of degradable fiberboard, remove it completely. Healthy soil doesn't contain enough moisture to effectively decompose such thick fiber, and if portions of the container inhibit root growth underground, the plant will quickly decline.

Fill the hole with enough soil mix to bring the shrub up to ground level, set the root ball in the hole and fill in with remaining soil. Using your hands, not your feet, firm the plant in, and then give it a deep drink of water. This is a crucial step in guaranteeing healthy growth for the plant. If the soil is compacted too firmly, fine pore spaces in the soil collapse and drive out oxygen. The plant is deprived of oxygen in the root zone, and growth never assumes normal vigor. It's always better to have a looser fit in the hole, rather than compact the soil too firmly around the root ball.

If the soil is compacted too firmly, fine pore spaces in the soil collapse and drive out oxygen.

You can add transplant fertilizer to the water for a quick growth start even if you've already mixed bonemeal into the soil. Woody shrubs don't require frequent or excessive fertilizer feeding. If grass surrounds the shrub, lawn fertilizer applied to the turf once or twice a year is sufficient for the grass and the shrub. Or a thick mulch of homemade garden compost or aged manure applied over the roots in spring will provide all the nourishment required to keep shrubs healthy and vigorous. In autumn, allow a generous layer of leaves to remain under and around the shrub. Leaves are the most natural form of plant food and also encourage earthworms to fertilize the soil with their castings.

How to Plant a Tree

mature. The roots of very large trees are mostly distributed in the top 36 inches (90 cm) of soil, where moisture and nutrients are available. If you've ever seen large trees "lifted" out of the soil by violent windstorms, you may have been surprised to see this saucer formation of the roots.

Soil preparation for tree planting is a bit different than it is for other plants. The hole should be just deep enough to equal the height of the root ball, and about twice as wide. Use a stiff tape measure to get the depth and width dimensions of the root ball. Trees require good drainage under their roots, so cover the bottom of the hole with 2 inches (5 cm) of coarse sand and use a garden fork to dig it in. Tamp the soil down with the back of a shovel, but don't tread on it with your feet. The addition of sand will raise the bottom of the hole slightly and help to drain water that might accumulate in the hole. Put half the excavated soil in a wheelbarrow or on a tarp, and amend it with organic materials and more coarse sand. Spread the other half of the original soil elsewhere in the garden.

If the tree is in a container, lay it on its side, grasp the trunk where it meets the soil and pull off the container. Press lightly on the container to help release

Woody plants that grow higher than 15 feet (4.5 m) are considered to be trees, no matter whether they have a single standard trunk or are multi-trunked and shrub-formed.

it, or cut it off and lift the tree into the hole. If the tree is large enough to have burlap wrap and also a wire basket, these coverings stay on and go into the hole. Unlike other woody plants, trees need to sit high in the saddle. The tree should be elevated approximately 1 to 2 inches (2.5–5 cm) above the grade of the soil; the sand dug into the bottom of the hole helps raise it up.

Once the tree is centered in the hole, bend the wire basket back and away from the top of the root ball, and untie the burlap. Pull the burlap away from the top of the root ball and use scissors to cut off as much as possible without exerting pressure or pulling. The bent-back basket and remaining burlap are buried. The basket continues to hold the root ball securely and protects it from shattering before roots have taken hold in the new soil; the burlap will decompose. Make sure the tree you purchase is wrapped in genuine burlap; synthetic burlap

Woody plants that grow higher than 15 feet (4.5 m) are considered to be trees, no matter whether they have a single standard trunk or are multi-trunked and shrub-formed. The height of these plants requires a broad root structure to keep them stable in the soil; despite popular mythology, trees seldom have deep taproots. Instead, they develop saucer-shaped root balls as they

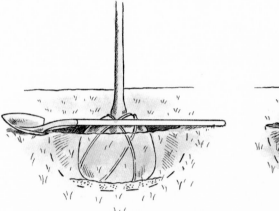

The hole should be just deep enough to equal the height of the root ball, and about twice as wide.

The tree should be elevated approximately 1 to 2 inches (2.5–5 cm) above the grade of the soil; the sand dug into the bottom of the hole helps raise it up.

has a shiny green appearance and won't degrade underground. If left in the hole, synthetic burlap may prevent roots from extending.

Fill in the rest of the hole with amended soil, covering the sides and top edges of the root ball, but leave the top section of the root ball closest to the trunk exposed. Firm the soil with the back of a shovel, and use your hands to form the extra soil into a saucer-shaped rim all around the hole to collect rain and irrigation water. Water the hole deeply, adding a transplant fertilizer if you wish. Trees planted in this manner require staking for their first year, until stabilizing roots have grown into the soil. Adding a 2-inch (5 cm) mulch of shredded bark

over the root ball helps conserve moisture and prevent sun and wind from dehydrating the root ball.

How to Stake a Tree

Incorrect staking deforms, mutilates and kills more trees than insects, disease and lightning do. Although tree trunks seem to be thick and unwieldy, they will struggle desperately to get away from a too-close stake. Tying a tree directly against a stake causes cells on the dark side of the trunk to lengthen as the tree bends into a bow shape to escape the shadow of the stake. Once this curvature develops, there is no setting it straight again, and structural problems follow as growth proceeds on the unbalanced structure. If the stake remains in place, bark eventually grows over the bindings, drawing them into the interior of the wood, where vital circulatory avenues are severed. Problems compound as wood dies and rotting diseases set in.

Trees over 8 feet (2.4 m) high need two stakes, placed on opposite sides of the trunk at the edge of the root ball. The pointed end of the stake should be driven into the soil outside of the root ball. Heavy wire is tightened around the stake, and an 8-inch (20 cm) length of rubber hose is slipped onto the wire and gently looped around the tree trunk. The hose section protects the bark from damage, and the wire is fastened back at the stake. Repeat the process with the stake on the opposite side. The purpose of the stakes isn't to hold the tree up but rather to prevent wind from rocking the root ball and tearing new roots. The pressure on the wires should be gently firm but not tight. Check every month to be sure the pressure continues to be correct, and remove the stakes after one to two years.

Remove storm and winter damage and finished flowers on plants such as the hydrangea.

Shrub care

Shrub borders are generally low-maintenance, but every kind of plant requires some basic care. Good drainage is essential for shrub growth; few shrubs can tolerate saturated soil. If necessary, improve drainage by digging in coarse builder's sand. Again, the planting hole can be enriched with composted manure (purchased in bags) to improve soil texture and encourage root growth. A liquid transplant solution with rooting hormone, purchased at the garden center, can also be provided (at the same time, with manure) to get shrubs growing quickly.

Chronic drought quickly degrades woody plants and ruins their ornamental capacity, so be sure to establish a regular watering schedule. Selecting plants with growth potential to fit the space available eliminates the need for most pruning, but storm and winter damage should be removed, and finished flowers cut off where possible. Conserving soil moisture with a 2-inch-thick (5 cm) organic mulch of leaves or shredded bark over all exposed soil also prevents weeds from getting a foothold in the bed. One trick to keeping a shrub border looking groomed and in pristine condition is to pay special attention to edging the bed with a sharp spade. Thirty minutes spent renewing the edge once a month makes the bed look as if it's had a full day of attention.

Few shrubs can tolerate water saturated soil. If necessary, improve drainage by digging in coarse builder's sand.

Best Early-Flowering Spring Shrubs

Flowering shrubs of every kind are useful and pleasing woody plants, but the most satisfying are those that bloom at the end of winter, just when gardeners are beginning to think there is no hope of spring. Early-blooming shrubs have flowers (some highly scented) that are unaffected by frosty nights or late snowfalls. In fact, they stay on the branches longer when temperatures remain cool to cold—a sudden flash of early warmth quickly terminates their blossoms.

If these early-flowering plants require pruning, be sure to wait until their flowers have finished or you will be removing their best ornamental features. Make any necessary pruning cuts immediately after the current year's flowers are finished to avoid cutting off next year's concealed flower buds.

1 Fragrant viburnum (*Viburnum farreri*)

H 10 feet (3 m) W 8 feet (2.5 m) –20°F (–29°C)
The earliest viburnum, this large shrub is loose and unkempt but has lovely pink panicle flowers and deeply veined foliage. It needs room to spread, but its very early scented blooms justify the space. Thin from the base each year to prevent it from consuming passersby. 'Nanum' is compact and neatly mounding, just 3 feet (1 m) high and perfect for a small garden. Part shade to full sun.

2 'PJM' rhododendron (*Rhododendron hybrid*)

H/W 4 feet (1.2 m) –30°F (–34°C)
This lepidote, or small-leafed, rhododendron is famously early and bright. Bright mauve-pink to lavender flowers that seem lit from within will shake up the early-spring garden. Autumn foliage is a beautiful mahogany with touches of scarlet, and the shrub doesn't require any winter wrapping as long as it's planted away from strong wind.

3 'Show Off' forsythia (*Forsythia* x *intermedia* 'Mindor')

H/W 5 feet (1.5 m) –30°F (–34°C)
A compact shrub with bright yellow flowers lining upright canes in early spring. Branches can be cut in late winter for indoor forcing. An even smaller dwarf forsythia is Sugar Baby (*F.* 'Nimbus') H 30 inches (75 cm). Full sun.

4 Tinkerbelle lilac (*Syringa* 'Bailbelle')

H/W 6 feet (1.8 m) –30°F (–34°C)
A compact lilac with wine-colored buds that open to scented pale pink flowers. Sister plants are similarly compact and include rosy-lilac Sugar Plum Fairy (*S.* 'Bailsugar') and lavender-pink 'Prince Charming.' No pruning required. Full sun.

5 Fragrant winter hazel (*Corylopsis glabrescens*)

H/W 15 feet (4.5 m) –20°F (–29°C)
This delicate and wide-spreading low shrub is well suited to a woodland garden. It produces fragrant, pale yellow flowers that dangle from the bare branches in an elegant early-spring display. The leaves are quite distinctive, broadly oval and deeply veined, turning yellow in autumn. An equally beautiful cousin is spike winter hazel (*C. spicata*). Part shade to full sun.

6 February Daphne (*Daphne mezereum*)

H 4 feet (1.2 m) W 3 feet (1 m) –30°F (–34°C)
Outstanding for fragrance in any season, place this by a doorway where the flowers can be appreciated in early spring. It may not bloom in February, but it will bloom early. In Ireland, flowers appear in January; in Ontario, they're out in March. The blue-green foliage is attractive all season, and inedible red berries appear in early autumn. White or pink-purple flowers. Part shade to full sun.

Best Plants for Autumn Display

It's easy to admire bright autumn color during the crisp days of winter's approach, but the time to plan for vivid foliage display is in spring, as days lengthen and warm. That is the time to strategically plant shrubs and trees that provide bursts of color at the end of the season. Select at least four plants with colorful autumn foliage from this list, and plant them in your garden where their impact will be visible.

Keep in mind that sunlight is a factor in the production of autumn leaf color. Some plants, like burning bush, must be placed in full sun to produce their crimson leaves. But Japanese maples of all kinds give good color with only half-day sun, as do many of the perennial cranesbill geraniums. Moisture is the second important factor; plants that have suffered from drought during midsummer won't be able to give their brightest effects in autumn. That's just another good reason for a reliable and sufficient irrigation program for every garden.

1 Japanese maple (*Acer palmatum*)

H 15 to 25 feet (4.5–7.6 m) –20°F (–29°C)

Dozens of species and hybrids are available, all producing vividly colored autumn foliage. 'Bloodgood' has the darkest burgundy leaf, with scarlet overtones in fall. 'Viridis' is a weeping shrub form with finely cut green leaves that turn orange in fall. Lesser known is purpleblow or Shantung maple (*Acer truncatum*), with miniature maple leaves that are reddish purple in spring, changing to glossy dark green, then glistening yellow-orange in autumn. Likes half-day sun and consistently moist, organic soil.

2 Dwarf fothergilla (*Fothergilla gardenii*)

H 36 inches (90 cm) W 24 inches (60 cm) –20 F (–29 C)

A compact refined shrub with fragrant white bottlebrush-like flowers in spring followed by blue-green rounded foliage. Autumn color is deep apricot-scarlet. 'Mount Airy' (*F. major* 'Mount Airy') H/W 5 feet (1.5 m) is yellow-orange-scarlet in fall. Prefers moist soil. Part shade to full sun.

3 Bluebeard (*Caryopteris* x *clandonensis*)

H 4 feet (1.2 m) –20°F (–29°C)

A small shrub with narrow, gray-green foliage and feathery blue flowers in late summer through early autumn. Darkest blue are 'Dark Knight' and 'Kew Blue'; 'Azure' is brighter, and 'Blue Mist' is powder-blue. Flowers best in sun with ordinary soil. Blue flowers appear on new wood of the current season. Wait until mid-spring to remove dead wood. Full sun.

4 Oakleaf hydrangea (*Hydrangea quercifolia*)

H 4 to 6 feet (1.2–1.8 m) –20°F (–29°C)

Like all hydrangeas, this bush grows well and flowers in partial sun. But in brighter light, the oak-like leaves take on vibrant autumn shades of red, orange-brown and purple. For spectacular autumn flowers, try *H. paniculata* Pinky Winky (*H. paniculata* 'DVP Pinky') and 'Fire and Ice' (*H. paniculata* 'Wim's Red'). Both have white flowers that turn vibrant pink in fall. Part shade to sun.

5 Burning bush, spindle tree (*Euonymus alatus*)

H/W 15 to 20 feet (4.5–6 m) –30°F (–34°C)

Burning scarlet foliage in autumn is this shrub's attraction. Smaller *E. alatus* 'Compactus' (5–8 ft/1.5–2.5 m) is similar and a good hedging plant that needs no pruning or shaping if planted 5 feet (1.5 m) apart. *E. europaeus* (H 12–30 ft/ 3.6–9 m) has deep pink and orange fruit from September to November. All need full sun to color up.

6 Ginkgo (*Ginkgo biloba*)

H 50 feet (15 m) –40°F (–40°C)

This ancient tree (also known as maidenhair tree) has unique foliage. Despite its height, it takes up relatively little room and doesn't cast shade for many decades. Drought-tolerant and pollution-resistant, it takes on a beautiful golden hue in autumn, lighting up a garden. The females, which produce malodorous fruit, are not sold commercially. Full sun.

Best Shrubs for Winter Interest

Gardeners who are easily seduced by flowers may need a bit of consciousness raising to recognize the ornamental features of plants in winter. In the absence of blossoms and foliage, woody shrubs are free to show their true character. After the fireworks of autumn color, the winter stems of burning bush are unexpectedly spangled with small, intensely red fruits. Double kerria carries a heavy burden of golden blooms in summer and then surprisingly reveals vivid apple-green stems in winter. Plants with ornamental winter features often have intriguing twig formation, like the corkscrew hazel, or dazzling red berries, like the highbush cranberry.

Placement is the important issue if ornamental winter features are to be best appreciated. Keeping plants with interesting architecture or colorful bark and fruits near doors and windows is the best way to enjoy them each day. It doesn't take many, and often just one is enough, but by placing winter interest plants close at hand, your garden truly becomes a year-round pleasure.

1 Redbark dogwood (*Cornus alba* 'Sibirica')

H/W 10 feet (3 m) −50°F (−45°C)
Green leaves in summer drop to reveal coral-red bark against winter snow. 'Flaviramea' is a bright yellow-stemmed variety, also with plain green leaves. 'Gouchaultii' has green, yellow and rose foliage carried on red stems. For best bark color, grow the shrubs in full sun, removing some older canes every year to encourage new wood.

2 Winterberry, deciduous holly (*Ilex verticillata*)

H/W 6 to 10 feet (1.8–3 m) −30°F (−34°C)
The species plant doesn't require a male pollinator and carries bunches of bright red fruits after its leaves drop. Hybrids, with larger berry clusters, need one male plant for up to six females and should be bought in matched sets: 'Jim Dandy' (M) with 'Afterglow' or 'Red Sprite' (F), and 'Southern Gentleman' (M) with 'Winter Red' (F). Full sun.

3 Highbush cranberry (*Viburnum trilobum*)

H/W 8 to 12 feet (2.5–3.6 m) −40°F (−40°C)
This is the most colorful of all the viburnums, with generous white flowers in spring, scarlet foliage in autumn and heavy, jewel-like fruits that last deep into winter. The clusters of deep scarlet berries become almost translucent in winter sun. Equally attractive is the dwarf *V. trilobum* 'Compactum' H/W 5 feet (1.5 m). Part shade to full sun.

4 Corkscrew hazel (*Corylus avellana* 'Contorta')

H/W 10 feet (3 m) −30°F (−34°C)
Intriguing in winter, with spiraled and corkscrewed twigs and silver-burnished wood. The catkin-like inflorescences lengthen through winter, opening into elegant tassels in spring. Grows in light shade to full sun, with more tassels and tighter corkscrews in a sunny location. Cut out any smooth or straight stems emerging from rootstock below the base.

5 Cranberry Cotoneaster (*Cotoneaster apiculatus*)

H 3 feet (1 m) W 5 feet (1.5 m) −30°F (−34°C)
A mounding, spreading shrub with dense, tightly held branches, this evergreen has pretty pink flowers in spring and striking red berries from late summer to fall, when its tiny dark green glossy leaves turn brick red. Often used for ground cover or as edging. Full sun to partial shade.

6 'Yukon Belle' scarlet firethorn (*Pyracantha angustifolia* 'Yukon Belle')

H/W 10 feet (3 m) −30°F (−34°C)
A broadleaf evergreen shrub with an upright and spreading posture and generous clusters of bright orange-red berries in winter. It should always be grown with a backdrop—a house corner, an entranceway door or a garden fence—so that it will be sheltered from winter wind. Cousin *P. coccinea* 'Chadwick' has arching branches. Full sun.

A Visit to the Garden Center

YOU'VE PREPARED A HOME FOR YOUR PLANTS BY CHOOSING the planting areas and preparing the beds. If your plan is to install shrubs or trees yourselves, you've pre-dug holes for them as well.

Your most important reference at this time is a thoughtfully researched shopping list of plants, fertilizers, tools, stakes and any other materials you anticipate to be necessary for making a swift and easy transfer of nursery plants to their permanent homes in your garden. You might want to divide planting operations into phases that can be accomplished over a series of long weekends or perhaps in periods of cool spring and autumn weather. Whatever number of phases you plan, be sure you can carry out the plant buying and installation jobs at that time, leaving nothing undone. No matter how modest the work you accomplish in any phase, a finished presentation will make your efforts shine.

Zone Guidelines

Before you start loading up your cart with plants, there's a key piece of information you need to have: all plants have a minimum temperature at which they can survive. Basically, that means gardeners in cold climates can't expect plants that thrive in warm climates like southern California to make it through the winter.

To help gardeners make selections that are appropriate for their area, the American and Canadian departments of agriculture have created climate maps dividing countries into zones 1 through 10. Each zone is assigned a range of temperatures indicating average minimum winter temperatures; colder zones, predictably, have lower numbers. See the maps on page 58.

At the garden center, a plant tag, in addition to indicating a plant's preference for sun or shade and its maximum height and width, should also indicate both the coldest zone and the coldest temperature in which that plant will thrive. Plants successful in your zone and in zones with numbers lower than yours should survive winters in your garden. Plants that prefer zones with higher numbers than yours may not be winter-hardy for you.

However, the reality is that conditions vary locally, and small microclimates may exist in your garden that are uncharacteristically warmer in winter. For instance, a foundation planting bed

Plant tag.

For winter interest, choose woody plants with ornamental berries and bark or a weeping form.

Garden centers generally won't sell a plant that isn't cold-hardy in your climate zone.

on a south-facing brick wall will be marginally warmer than a planting bed farther out in the garden. You can also expect the effects of climate change to occasionally create warmer winters, but that may be canceled out by unexpectedly severe periods of ice and snow.

To ensure a plant is winter-hardy in your garden, you need to know the minimum coldest winter temperature in your region. Garden centers generally won't sell a plant that isn't cold-hardy in your climate zone, and the garden-center staff should be able to tell you what hardiness zone you're in. You can also check the USDA and Canadian hardiness zone maps through a simple Internet search and then confidently select plants with hardiness ratings that at least correspond to your minimum coldest temperature. As an example, if your garden's temperature falls to minus 20 degrees F (−29°C) every winter, you are in USDA Zone 5. When selecting plants, be sure that they are hardy to USDA Zone 4 or lower. If you attempt to put plants hardy only to USDA Zone 6 (−10°F/−23°C) into the garden, there is a good chance you will lose them to frost damage.

Several zone guidelines are used in North America, and it can be confusing to know which one to follow. What is most important is to know the minimum low winter temperature in your garden, and then check that against the hardiness rating of plants before you purchase them. For clarity, we've included temperatures rather than zone numbers with our plant lists. Don't purchase plants that aren't evaluated for cold hardiness.

Buyer Be Wary

Hygiene is an important factor in nurseries and indicates the level of care and good cultural practices that are taken to prevent problems. The outsides of perennial pots should be relatively clean, and the pots should not be left sitting in a muddy tray. Nor should weeds be sprouting up alongside the plant. If the garden center has enough staff to water plants regularly, you should never see pots that are completely dry. Lifting and feeling the weight of a pot will tell you if it has been adequately watered—if the pot feels light, it contains dry soil. When plants are allowed to dry out and wilt repeatedly, their growth is interrupted and may not resume that season, and they become targets for insects and disease. Plant foliage should be a consistent green color without yellow patches or spots, and the leaves should have good turgidity, a firm resilience indicating that the root system is moving water efficiently up the stems. You can check turgidity by gently depressing a leaf and watching it spring back into position. If it doesn't spring back, something's wrong.

If you notice insects on plants, at least you know they haven't been sprayed recently and are safe to touch. Typically, you'll see sucking insects like spittlebugs and aphids that are easily removed with a spray of water at home. (Another efficient method of removing a few insects is by hand-picking. A pair of "bug-dedicated" rubber gloves will embolden even the most squeamish.) But if the undersides of leaves show a collection of tiny white flies, that's a problem to be avoided: whiteflies are difficult to suppress and breed very rapidly, and you don't want to bring them home and introduce them to your garden. Needless to say, any plants with mushy or spotted leaves are diseased; they shouldn't even be offered for sale.

Room to Grow

Using a liquid transplant solution purchased at the garden center is the best way to get plants off to a vigorous growing start. Transplant solution contains fertilizer and a rooting hormone that encourages plants to begin growing roots into their new holes as soon as they're planted.

From spring through early summer, perennial plants increase

You should never see pots that are completely dry. Lifting and feeling the weight of a pot will tell you if it has been adequately watered—if the pot feels light, it contains dry soil.

Avoid plants with a collection of tiny whiteflies on the underside of leaves. Whiteflies are difficult to suppress.

Getting Started

A spring afternoon at a garden center can unsettle the most ardent shopper, assuming you manage to find a space in the parking lot. On the way in, you're distracted by something wonderful in full bloom in someone's cart, but no one knows its name. You've come to purchase forsythia, yet there are six varieties to choose from. The only employee with plant information hasn't been seen for some time. You want to stock up on columbines, but everything is organized by botanical names and you never took Latin. The checkout line takes 20 minutes to clear, and all you bought are gloves. What's wrong with this picture?

A friendly piece of advice: Don't wait for the first nice warm day to visit the garden center; everyone else will have the same idea. Nurseries begin bringing in plants at the end of winter, and they welcome early business. A cold, wet and windy day is often the best time to peruse the plants, get quick service and see the best selection of plants that may be scarce later in the season. To be alone and unhurried in the nursery aisles is not only a rare form of pleasure but also an opportunity to concentrate on the matter at hand.

When you do make the trip, consider bringing along a few practical items.

1. Lightweight Gardening Gloves

So much plant material gathered in one place is an opportunity for many kinds of pests to proliferate, and some nurseries guard against plant damage by spraying pesticides. Wholesale suppliers spray plants with pesticides in the growing fields and before they're delivered. But you won't know about it while you're walking the aisles, so wear the gloves. If you haven't got gloves, keep your hands away from your face and wash them when you get home.

2. A Few Large Plastic Bags

Spread the bags on the car floor or trunk to protect your car from any loose soil that might spill from the plant containers. If you're bringing home shrubs in large pots, put each pot into a plastic bag of its own, then lay the shrub carefully on its side, bolstering it with other pots and containers to prevent rolling.

3. A Good Plant Encyclopedia

Purchasing plants requires a strategy. Some plant families are very large, and you may need to know both the common name and the Latin botanical name to get exactly what you're after. As an example, autumn crocus is also known as meadow saffron and naked lady, but the correct

Shade Plants

Full Sun Plants

botanical name is *Colchicum autumnale*. Garden-center staff may be confused by multiple common names, but knowing the correct botanical name will always get you the exact plant you want. Often there's only one person at the center trained in horticulture, and that person never seems to be where you need him or her to be. Inevitably, you will find an intriguing plant that you'd like to know more about. Ideally, it will have an identifying tag on it, and you'll be able to find out what you want to know by consulting your handy reference. Consider purchasing simple plant guides like Ortho's *All About Perennials* and Ortho's *Complete Guide to Trees and Shrubs*, and bring them to the garden center with you.

Of course, in our digital world, you could also use a smart phone or a tablet to research a plant and its characteristics while at the garden center. There are a host of reliable online sites, some of them garden centers themselves, that provide relevant information about habits and hardiness.

Looking at plants in a nursery is a little like visiting cats and dogs at the pound—you're not seeing them in the best circumstance or at their full potential. But if you know what you want and can recognize a good specimen when you see it, you're ahead of the game.

their size by growing more roots, expanding from the crown and putting up more stems. If you get the plants you bought at the garden center into the ground early in the season, they will put on good growth their first year in your garden. If you wait until midsummer, you'll probably lose a year's worth of growth.

Perennials sold in 4-inch (10 cm) pots are unlikely to put up more than a token blossom the first year but will enlarge their crowns and flower well in the second growing season. If you want a perennial to bloom the first year, you'll have to purchase larger (and more expensive) plants in gallon containers. The number of growing points sprouting from the crown is an indication of the number of flowers that plant will produce. Plants with multiple growing points are good bargains and can usually be divided at the end of the first season, which will give you several small plants from one big specimen.

Plant sizes and pricing are fairly consistent between nurseries, so hunting for a bargain is probably a waste of time. Reduced prices in spring or summer may indicate something amiss in the nursery. But it is possible to find reductions toward the end of the season and through to the autumn, when garden centers try to sell off as much stock as possible to reduce their winter storage costs. The selection is more limited, and these plants have spent a long, hot season in containers, but they can be rehabilitated with tender loving care, and you might find some good buys.

You should be able to tell from the condition of the foliage whether the root system is still in good working order. Large trees and shrubs are the big-ticket items in any season, and if their root balls are big enough to require a wire basket wrapping, you'll know that's where the money is. A large root ball and thick trunk are indicators of maturity and the length of time the tree has been held before sale. Since trees produce a new layer of bark each year of their lives, tree value is measured by the width of the trunk and not by height. Vertical growth is sporadic and slows down or accelerates at different stages of development; it is also directly affected by cultural practices. For example, when grown in soils deficient in oxygen, moisture and fertility, trees will slow both trunk diameter and vertical growth and have dead twigs throughout. When selecting a tree, choose a stocky specimen

If you want a perennial to bloom the first year, you'll have to purchase larger (and more expensive) plants in gallon containers.

Balled and burlapped trees should be planted as soon as possible and their root balls kept wet until then.

with a thicker trunk over a slender and tall tree. Once planted, the shorter specimen will make noticeable upward growth.

Woody plants can tell you a lot about themselves. The bark shows the pruning history of the plant, and you can find the places where wood has been removed as it grew. If old seed heads still cling to twigs or can be found around the trunk in the pot, you know the plant is mature enough to bloom. That can be valuable information if you're looking at lilac or wisteria, which won't flower if too young. If you want to be sure of the exact color of a plant's blooms, purchase it when it's in flower.

The woody scaffold shows the front and back of the plant as it responded to its light placement in the nursery. The back is the darkest side and will be flat, while branches at the front have had more light and are fuller. This shows you how to face the plant outward when you set it into a hole.

Clean pruning scars that heal quickly are no problem, but watch for ragged or rough-gouged injuries in the wood, particularly if you're purchasing a tree. The ragged edges of accidental damage are slow to heal and allow disease organisms to enter, infecting the interior wood. Some nurseries wrap a protective sheath of corrugated paper or plastic around tree trunks to prevent damage, and that should be removed after planting.

Read the Fine Print

Gardeners often assume all plants purchased at a nursery are guaranteed. They're right about that, but it's important to understand just what the guarantee covers and for how long.

Generally, nurseries sell only plants that are winter-hardy in their region and guarantee the plants won't die from cold over the first winter. The guarantee doesn't cover insect and disease damage, the effects of drought, poor planting practices, fertilizer burn or any other kind of owner abuse.

Large garden centers may replace the dead carcass of any toasted plant you take back in spring, no questions asked; smaller nurseries might ask about how you looked after the plant. You can avoid this embarrassment by making sure all your plants have the best of everything.

When selecting a tree, choose a stocky specimen with a thicker trunk over a slender and tall tree.

Traveling with Plants

A shopping spree at the garden center can lead to moments of panic in the parking lot. How can three cartloads of plants possibly fit into a compact car? It's not an easy puzzle to solve, but you can try. It's better to shop alone, because people take up a lot of room in the car. Also, if you have bought tall plants, it helps if you have a back seat that folds flat. Some nurseries supply plastic to protect car upholstery, but think about keeping a small plastic tarp, large garbage bags, old bed sheets or blankets, a roll of jute twine and scissors in the trunk for these occasions.

Garden centers offer delivery with their truck but may charge a substantial fee for the service. If staff are available, they'll even help load a few heavy containers into the trunk, but remember that you'll also need help getting them out at home. And staff won't be able to cope with elaborate packing jobs when you've purchased a small forest. If you're going to attempt the transport yourself, begin with the largest and heaviest plants. Tie the jute twine around the branches of shrubs, lightly compressing their shape to prevent twig damage. Every place in the car is useful for packing plants except the driver's seat, so open the trunk and all the doors. Put shrubs in head first, with the heavy container ends closest to the trunk and door openings to make removal easier.

Try to line up containers so they'll support each other. Bags of manure can be laid between or on top of heavy containers for bracing. Tall plants may have to be put into the trunk diagonally or straight across the back seat. It's all right if twiggy plant bodies overlap each other so long as their heavy bottoms are stationary. It won't hurt the top twigs of a tall plant if they're gently bent for the duration of the trip. Use gallon-sized pots of perennial plants to fill in the gaps between larger containers to prevent rolling.

If plants must protrude slightly from windows or from the trunk, cover or wrap the exposed parts. High-speed wind will desiccate buds and shrivel leaves and evergreens quickly. Bring along old pillowcases, and tie them over exposed parts. The back-seat footwells are good places for tall perennials with tender stems. If a passenger is riding in front, he or she can manage a small shrub between the legs and hold a tray of annuals or small perennials. Tighten the caps of liquid fertilizers and put them,

along with books and hand tools, under the front seats, and you're ready to buckle up and hit the road. Don't mind the stares, and take it easy on turns.

Temporary Storage

Getting the best selection means shopping early, so you may end up purchasing plants before the garden site is ready for installation. The plants can stay in their containers for a few weeks if you're conscientious about keeping them healthy. Garden-center staff have given them daily attention, so you can pick up where they left off. It's important to keep plants in a shady location with protection from wind. Even in cool weather, direct sunlight can seriously stress plants and check growth. Black plastic containers heat up quickly, cooking plant roots and disrupting delivery of water to stems and leaves. If there's any danger of frost at night, take plants into an unheated garage; or if that's not possible, carefully arrange a blanket over them until morning. Large plants that are balled and burlapped need to be heeled in with their root balls temporarily protected (see Heeling In, right).

The gardener's job is to make sure soil is moist and pots feel heavy each day. Perennials grown in peat-based soil mixes dry

If you're using plastic bags for temporary plant storage, it's crucial to punch drainage holes in the bottoms.

Heeling In

If you need to hold the plant for a while before getting it in the ground, it will need to be heeled in somewhere. Dig a shallow depression in a shady spot and set the root ball in it, then cover the exposed portion with the contents of a purchased bag of shredded bark, and keep it wet. If you've no area where this is possible, you can put the root ball and the shredded bark in a large plastic garbage bag and prop it up in a shady corner. Poke drainage holes in the bottom of the bag, and keep the root ball damp but not dripping.

Plants in containers can wait a while for planting as long as they are watered and stored in the shade.

out quickly and may be hard to re-wet. Watering them with hot tap water will reactivate the absorbing action. Large or small containers that are very dry can be stood in a bucket of hot water for an hour and will rapidly take up the warm drink.

Ground-cover plants are the least tolerant of temporary storage while waiting for a hole of their own. They want to make horizontal growth outward, and their root systems begin to expand early in spring. They deteriorate more rapidly as roots press against the sides of containers and are frustrated in their growth process. If you must hold ground covers for more than two weeks, it might be a good idea to transplant them into larger pots or find a temporary place in the ground where they can wait.

Staying On

Sometimes, it's love at first sight: you're so taken with your new house that there's a chance it will be your forever home. In turn, there's also a chance that your first garden may be your forever garden. With that in mind, you may want to take a longer look at potential landscape plans. Knowing you may enjoy your landscape plan over decades will almost certainly change the decisions you make today.

Ground-cover plants are the least tolerant of temporary storage while waiting for a hole of their own.

The first consideration is the financial investment required to create a landscape that will grow in beauty and usefulness. Longer-range plans may increase the budget, but remember: You don't have to spend it all in one season. With the luxury of time, you can plan landscape developments in phases, taking several years to reach a fully implemented design of your property. If you know that you'll stay in the house long enough to enjoy

Your First Garden